SLIM CHANCES

A True Story of Struggle, Hope, and Forgiveness

Mirabel,

Thank you for your support!
I hope you like my book.

Jimmy "Slim" Rumsey

www.slimchancesbook.com

ISBN: 9780578897691

DEDICATION

This book is dedicated to the lost, the abandoned, the unloved, those struggling, and those otherwise forgotten. It was written to remind people that everyone deserves a second chance no matter the circumstances. You have the power to turn your life around. Hope is on your side.

CONTENTS

FOREWORD

Jeff "Pac-Man" Blair – Tustin Deputy Chief of Police

I was born and raised in Tustin, California, located in the center of Orange County. Growing up as a teenager in Tustin, I never had to concern myself with being targeted for crime, avoiding bad parts of town, or worrying about being confronted by gang members. But things changed drastically in the late 1980s.

By the time I was sworn in as a Tustin Police Officer in 1989 at the ripe age of 20, my hometown looked very different than it had just a few short years earlier. The popular movie about gangs in Los Angeles called *Colors* had just been released, and the Hollywood influence over the youth was evident. Some teenagers who were a few years younger than me began a break-dancing club at Tustin High School the year I graduated in 1986. By the time I became a cop three years later, that break-dancing club had become a street gang known as the Duce Tray Crips.

Initially, the gang was racially mixed but definitely influenced by the African American Crips gangs from South Central Los Angeles, which is a short drive north on Interstate 5. Driving through southwest Tustin, dozens of teenagers wore baggy jeans, British Knight (BK) tennis shoes, blue Pendleton jackets, and navy bandannas.

Alleys and street corners were covered with 2x3 Crips graffiti that often read like a roster for the Duce Tray Crips— Sleepy, Midnight, Troop, Bear, Brain, C-Rocc, UZI-K, Big

Stuff, Thumper. This was usually followed by a message to enemies like "BK 187" which, translated, meant Blood Killers and murder.

I quickly realized these gangsters were not just making a fashion statement. They were out committing crimes on a regular basis. As a patrol cop, I was responding to gang fights, residential burglaries, automobile thefts, and assaults.

For me to become a productive street cop, I knew I had to learn as much about gangs as possible, so I immersed myself in learning the inner workings of the subculture. The gangsters on the street had even dubbed me "Pac-Man," named after the Sean Penn character in the movie, *Colors.*

Crime in Tustin and throughout all of Orange County was skyrocketing. Gangs were getting blamed for the spike. The heart of the Duce Tray Crips' "turf" was the intersection of McFadden Avenue and Pasadena Avenue, where a small strip mall was located, surrounded by high-density apartments.

One year, there was a murder on all four corners of that intersection such that the local newspaper dubbed it "Tustin's Killer Corner." On the west side of McFadden and the 55 Freeway overpass was Tustin Village Way. It was a perfect location to park our squad cars to see exactly who was coming into and leaving our city.

It was the main thoroughfare that led to Minnie Street in Santa Ana, which, at the time, was a well-known location to purchase crack cocaine or heroin. I had made so many gun arrests conducting routine traffic stops that the intersection was jokingly referred to as the "gat checkpoint" by our officers.

While working night shifts, I would often broadcast over the radio, "34-301. 961. Gat Check," to inform my dispatcher I was conducting a traffic stop at the intersection of McFadden and Tustin Village Way.

By the early-mid 1990s, there were several active gangs in the city. Los Wickeds had established a stronghold in an isolated area of the city just west of the 55 freeway. The Laurel Hood Thugs (LHT) gang had formed in a fairly nice residential area on the east side of town. A new gang known as Barrio Brown Revolution (BBR) was establishing itself in a run-down apartment complex on the outskirts of Old Town Tustin.

Even tagger crews such as Bombsquad (BSD) and Never Stopped Killing (NSK) were morphing into criminal street gangs. In addition to our home-grown gangs, there were splinter gangs from the adjacent city, Santa Ana, that were operating in our town—Southside, Dogtown, Middleside, Little Minnie Street, and the Alley Boys, to name a few.

Generally speaking, these were traditional Hispanic street gangs. One non-traditional gang that didn't necessarily claim an area was a new Filipino gang known as Alpha Kappa Rho or AKP for short. They came out of nowhere and seemed to be everywhere. In gang terms, they were "deep."

To complicate matters, AKP also went by the name Alpha Kappa PIRU which meant they were Bloods – sworn enemies of the Crips. Make no mistake, the Duce Tray Crips were still the apex predator of gangs in Tustin, but AKP members were shooters. Bullets were flying in both directions.

For several years, city leaders and even police department leaders tried to minimize the gangs' presence and their impact in Tustin. The common theme was to point out that neighboring cities such as Santa Ana and Orange had gang problems, not Tustin. But after a few more high-profile murders—including a cold-blooded afterhours stabbing on the tennis courts of Tustin High School—police and city leaders decided to take a stand.

In 1996, the Tustin Police Department Gang Unit was formed, and I was selected to be a founding member. I had been tracking gangs in our city since my rookie year so I knew I was the right guy for the job.

My partners were carefully selected, full of energy, and ready to make an impact. In total, there were five of us and we were the proverbial "tip of the spear" in the war on gangs. I had complete confidence in my partners: Stumpy, Rox, Bull, and many others. We cruised the streets of southwest Tustin in an undercover Cadillac Coupe De Ville that had been confiscated during a large-scale narcotics transportation operation. Our impact was immediate and extremely effective.

The Tustin Gang Unit targeted the worst of the worst. In 1996, no gang caused as much chaos as the Duce Tray Crips. They were public enemy #1. By this time the gang had weeded out weaker members so those who were still active were considered "riders" (hardcore).

The gang had about 40 or so members in Tustin and most were black, with very few exceptions. To be an "exception" you had to be extra dedicated to the gang — extra crazy and willing to do things others would not. That is exactly how I would describe Jimmy Rumsey. Jimmy was the only white member of the Duce Tray Crips. He was tall and rail thin, which is why he was known on the streets as "Slim."

Even though we were tenacious in our quest to crack down on Duce Tray, they were equally dedicated to imposing their will upon other gangs through fear and violence.

They had become so brazen with their gangbanging that they were making a lot of enemies from local gangs and neighboring cities alike. The graffiti changed from "BK 187" to "ABK 187" which was their message that they were "anybody killers."

This eventually led them to start a beef with Orange County's biggest black gang, Santa Ana's Watergate Crips. When we responded to calls of shots being fired, we knew the majority of the time it was the Duce Tray Crips on the giving or receiving end of the gun. The common denominator was Jimmy Rumsey. Jimmy had been shot at more times than I can exactly remember, but I know for a fact he was targeted at least four times because I was involved in every investigation.

I was there the day he was shot at on Red Hill Avenue and his passenger was struck in the back courtesy of AKP. I was there the day he and his fellow gangsters were sprayed with bullets in a drive-by shooting on Mitchell Avenue. Jimmy was lucky because somehow the bullets always missed their mark.

We knew taking down Duce Tray would not be easy, so we employed a variety of tactics. We used surveillance, served search warrants, and even had informants feeding us information. We learned the reason Jimmy was being targeted so frequently was that he was "putting in the most work" for the gang, which meant he was out committing crimes on behalf of the gang.

Despite being targeted by his rivals so frequently, and despite us pulling out all the stops, Jimmy always skated. We knew he was trigger-happy and foolhardy, and yet, somehow, we could never catch him dirty. Because of this, we dubbed him "Teflon Jimmy." Nothing would ever stick to him—not our cases or attacks from rivals.

In the meantime, Duce Tray members were catching some heavy cases. A big break for us occurred when they attacked one of their own members and he decided to cooperate with us. That led to "Operation Blue Rag," where we led a multi-agency gang sweep that netted five arrests for felony assault charges. That case drew heavy press attention and gave us some momentum.

Next, we arrested three newer members of the gang after they shot a rival in the back with a sawed-off shotgun on Alliance Avenue. We arrested two more for a carjacking near Tustin High School. Still, the crimes committed by Duce Tray continued to escalate. Three more were arrested for stabbing one of their own members to death during a gang "jump out" on the Marine Corps air station, El Toro.

A short time later, the Santa Ana Police arrested four Duce Tray leaders for committing a drive-by shooting across the street from the Santa Ana Zoo on the Santa Ana/Tustin border.

At one point, there were over 20 Duce Tray Crips in the Orange County Jail when I received a call from an Orange County Sheriff Gang Classification Officer who was listing them as a "disruptive group" inside the jail system. That is essentially one step away from being identified as a prison gang. Despite all the bedlam, violence and arrests, Teflon Jimmy Rumsey was still free on the streets "putting in the work."

On October 4, 1997, I was at home sleeping when I got a phone call. It was the Tustin Police Department Watch Commander informing me there had just been a gang shooting and that I needed to respond immediately because the victim was likely going to die. I asked who had been shot. He answered, "A kid named Rumsey. He took a large caliber bullet to the face."

I remember driving, thinking that Teflon Jimmy was no longer Teflon and that it was no coincidence that he would find his fate at Tustin's Killer Corner. When I got to the hospital, things looked grim. Jimmy looked like a typical gunshot victim in his final moments.

Of course, we did our best to communicate with him and record a dying declaration, but even on death's doorstep, Jimmy would not cooperate with us. The strange thing is that I had a very good idea about which gang was responsible for shooting him because things had been escalating rapidly between their main rivals from Santa Ana at the time.

I had seen the graffiti taunts back and forth as each would creep into the rival's neighborhood to spray paint threats against each other. I knew it would only be a matter of time before they bumped into each other, and I knew violence would follow.

In the weeks that followed, Jimmy's condition began to improve. I remember thinking that it was one thing to escape jail, but another to escape death. We had an informant tell us exactly who did it, but we needed a positive identification from a witness.

We tried to work Jimmy in every way possible to get him to identify the gunman, but he stayed true to the gang rule book and refused to cooperate with us. I knew he was going to handle this on his terms and revenge would come from a bullet, not a jury. Despite our bull-dogged efforts, Jimmy's attackers were lucky to *get away*.

For the next few months, Duce Tray laid low. I had not seen Jimmy and had heard he moved to Riverside County. We were focusing our enforcement efforts on some of the other gangs that had stepped up their activities. So, although we stayed busy, Duce Tray was no longer a top priority.

Then, in the early evening hours of April 1998, my Gang Unit partner, Duane Havourd, and I were on patrol in the area of El Camino Real and Tustin East Drive when we spotted a speeding vehicle. We could not see inside the car, so we had no idea who the occupants were, but we decided to conduct a routine traffic stop for the speeding violation.

Upon contact with the occupants, we immediately recognized them as Duce Tray Crips. The driver was not hardcore, more of a wannabe, but the passengers were diehard members—Slim was one of them!

I was shocked to see Jimmy Rumsey sitting in the back seat with his jaw wired shut and about 20 pounds lighter than his already thin frame usually carried. I saw that the car stereo had a bullet hole in it. On the floorboard, there was a shell casing. And in the glovebox, there was a loaded semi-automatic .22 caliber pistol.

The driver went on to finger Jimmy as the owner of the gun and he told a tale of a drunken Jimmy firing a round into the stereo because he didn't like the song being played. Jimmy was drunk, armed, and looking for payback, but we caught him before he could find his rivals.

Finally, I had a strong felony charge against Jimmy.

He had a colorful juvenile record, but he managed to avoid being charged with anything heavy since becoming an adult. I knew Jimmy would struggle in jail due to the racial politics and the number of enemies he had accumulated during his years of terrorizing rival gang members. I figured this would be the last I saw of Jimmy. In my mind, he would either end up dead or in prison for the rest of his life.

In the summer of 2015, almost two decades after the formation of our Gang Unit, *Behind the Badge* filed a story about the whereabouts of our original members. It featured a photograph of me and my former partner, walking through the alley of Alliance Avenue reminiscing about the "hot years" of the 1990s.

A few days after the article was published, I received an email from an address I did not recognize. The subject of the email was "Killer Corner Survivor." I opened the email and saw a message from Jimmy Rumsey.

I had not seen or heard from Jimmy a single time since that arrest in 1998. His message to me was that he quit the gang life and was a proud husband and parent. He included a photograph of his beautiful family and boasted that his daughter had just accepted a scholarship to attend college in Hawaii. Jimmy said he would love to meet for a cup of coffee to discuss ways that he could help reach out to the youth of Tustin in a positive manner through gang and drug intervention. I was shocked, to say the least.

Behind the Badge heard about the email and decided to send a crew to cover the meeting. When Jimmy arrived, he looked more like an accountant than a former gang member. In speaking to Jimmy, I could tell the man he had become was nothing like the kid he used to be. He truly wanted to contribute to the community in a positive way. It was almost as if he sensed a duty to pay amends for all the bad things he had done in his youth.

I am suspicious by nature, as all good cops should be, but Jimmy's intentions were pure. I told him I would support him in his efforts, but that he had to be the one out there "putting in the work." This time the work would not be for the benefit of the gang. Instead, it would be to save kids from making the same mistakes he and other gang members like him had made.

It has been a few years since that meeting and Jimmy is now a Restorative Practice Intervention Specialist. When he told me that he was writing a book and asked me to write the foreword, I was honored. I figure that if Jimmy can turn his life around, others can too.

PROLOGUE

When he pulled out the gun and pointed it at me, I didn't flinch. I didn't even think about running away. I just stood there staring down the barrel of the gun.

It wasn't out of fear that I froze. At that point in my life, I didn't care if I died. My eyes met his. *Go ahead, do it.*

He pulled the trigger.

When the bullet pierced through the front of my chin, I fell backward and smacked my head on the sidewalk. As I lay on the concrete, blood filled my mouth. I couldn't breathe. I was drowning in my own blood.

All my life choices culminated in this very moment—the moment I received a .38 caliber bullet to the face at close range. It's hard to explain, but many things raced through my mind when I was near death. What I remember the most was thinking of my two daughters. I kept seeing their smiling faces. I didn't want to leave them without a father. It was at that moment that I realized I had something to live for. I wasn't ready to die.

I wanted more time to live. I wanted more time with my family. I wanted more time to break free from the struggle, the trauma, and the pain. I wanted more time to change my ways. I wanted the opportunity to give my children a good life.

A split-second before I lost consciousness, I thought, *if only I had a second chance...*

Chapter 1

BORN ON THE RUN

If my life were a movie, the opening scene would show a young, naïve woman running out of her high school and jumping onto the back of a Harley Davidson motorcycle with a fearless outlaw. The driver would be a member of a notorious California biker gang who lived a life of drugs, alcohol, and crime. Soon after meeting each other, these two people would fall in love and, shortly after that, they would become my parents.

My dad and mom often spent their time on the Harley, speeding along one of California's famous highways on the Pacific Coast overlooking the ocean. They didn't know where they were going, but it didn't matter—they didn't have a care in the world. A few months later, this idyllic image of my parents and their carefree way of living would fade away in the rearview mirror as my dad was arrested and my mom became pregnant with me.

In the winter of 1975, when my dad and his biker friends were having a house party, some uninvited guests showed up. For whatever reason, my dad attacked one of them with a knife. Decades later, as I was putting the pieces of my life story together, my mom shared with me an old newspaper article from *The Los Angeles Times*. The headline read, "Man Knifed at Party in West Valley." I wasn't so shocked to know that my dad's crime made it into the newspaper, but I was surprised that my mom had held onto the original newspaper article for four decades. It read:

A 24-year-old Woodland Hills man was booked on suspicion of assault with intent to commit murder in connection with the stabbing of a 21-year-old man of Los Angeles at a party in Canoga Park. West Valley Area investigators said James Morgan Rumsey was arrested at the scene of the stabbing Friday night. Witnesses told police that Rumsey reportedly stabbed the 21-year-old several times in the chest on the front lawn of the home.

As soon as my dad bailed out of jail, he and my mom decided to flee the country. After trading in his Harley Davidson for a car, they headed northeast. With my mom by his side, my half-sister, Sheree, in the back seat, and me riding shotgun in my mom's womb, life on the run began.

Without a plan, my dad and mom sped across the border into Canada. While on their journey, they slept in their car or camped in the woods. Once they made it to the most eastern part of Canada, my dad ditched the car, bought a sailboat, and taught himself how to sail. Soon after our arrival, I was born at Grace Maternity Hospital in Halifax, Nova Scotia. Because my mom was only seventeen years old and still a kid herself, she was terrified of childbirth, not knowing what to expect. To make matters worse, my dad prevented her from seeing a doctor during her pregnancy because of his fear of tipping off authorities.

When my mom went into labor, they were living on the sailboat in Halifax. My dad somehow managed to get her to the hospital to give birth. This was the first and last time she saw a doctor related to her pregnancy. As soon as a physician medically cleared us to leave the hospital, we were gone.

From there, life consisted of hasty decisions based on my dad's paranoia of being caught for fleeing the US. My mom later told me that my dad lied to everyone about who we were and why we were living in Canada.

From the day I was born, everything my parents did was to evade law enforcement. For this reason, it was too dangerous for my dad to get close to strangers. He couldn't risk someone finding out where we came from, what we were doing there, or where we were going next. If anyone tried to befriend us, he pulled the family away.

Part of our family's survival meant continuing an ongoing act of assumed identities and fabricated stories. Moving from place to place made it difficult for me and my half-sister to keep those identities and stories straight. It would be roughly twenty years before I discovered that I was a Canadian citizen by birthright and that I was born under the alias of James Connor. Later, I would have my name legally changed to James Rumsey.

In the beginning, my mom was in love with my dad, and that love made it easier for her to follow him, but their relationship began to unravel as they felt the struggles associated with living on the run. My dad was verbally abusive and sometimes violent towards my mom. He often took his frustration out on her. My mom was alone with a fugitive, in another country, with no money, and with no place to go. She continued to tolerate the abuse because she felt that she had no way out.

While in Canada, our sailboat was our primary mode of transportation and provided us a place to live—mainly because it was cheap and allowed us to go unnoticed. Living on the sailboat kept my dad from being caught.

We spent most of our time traveling north and south along the eastern seaboard of North America. Where we traveled was entirely up to my dad. When he was ready to go, we went. When he determined it was safe to stay, we stayed. According to him, the next place we landed would be wherever we were "meant to be."

He must have decided it was safe to live on the land for a while as he moved us into an apartment for a short time in Brooklyn, New York. I learned from my mom that I had almost died from sudden infant death syndrome while living in that apartment. My dad found me in my crib, appearing to suffocate, with my face turning blue. He rushed me to the hospital and carried my limp body into the emergency room, screaming and yelling at the doctors to save me.

Soon after that, we were on the move again, this time to New Jersey. We stayed in New Jersey until I was three years old. While we were there, Mom gave birth to my sister, Della. We set sail shortly after Della was born and headed south to Florida.

While in Florida, my dad sold the boat, and we found a little house in St. Petersburg. When we landed in our new "home of the moment," as Mom called it, we walked wherever we needed to go or relied on public transportation when we could afford it. My dad worked odd jobs because he couldn't hold down a nine-to-five job. He also supported the family by scamming people out of money.

For a while, he placed advertisements in the classified section of a local newspaper to sell an old car. When someone would show up to purchase the car, he'd somehow come home with their money although he did not give them a car. He also got to know locals around the docks just enough to gamble with them. He was skilled at cheating them out of their money. Eventually, he got caught and we were on the move again.

To support the family, my mom started engaging in similar criminal behaviors. She and my dad would both shoplift for groceries. She was never as good as my dad, and it wasn't long before she got arrested for stealing. After a short stint in jail, she was released.

Things continued to get worse between my parents. My mom was always afraid that my dad would run off with me and Della if he had any inkling that my mom was unhappy with him and wanted to leave him. As these thoughts weighed heavier and heavier on my mom, she panicked and quickly devised a plan to run away from my dad before he had the chance to abduct us from her. My mom sought help from a local church and spoke to her parents in Los Angeles. When the time was right and he was working, she dropped off Sheree with a babysitter, packed up our things in black garbage bags, and scribbled a note in lipstick on the bathroom mirror. She wrote in large, bold red letters, "I'm leaving you."

Mom arranged a ride to the nearby airport where her mom had plane tickets waiting for us. The three of us were heading back to California.

Chapter 2

CALIFORNIA DREAMIN'

My mom was thankful to leave her troubles behind—and by "troubles," I mean my dad. California was the only home she had known and, with other family members also living there, she thought it would be the best place for us to get a new start. Fortunately, she would have her mom to rely on for financial support.

I hadn't realized that living on a boat in the ocean was abnormal. It was all I had known. I didn't understand that it was my mom's goal for me to never see my dad or Sheree again. As I got older, I'd ask my mom about Sheree and my dad's whereabouts. She'd always reply, "Your dad is dead or in prison, and I have no idea what happened to his daughter." For many years, I just assumed that what she told me was the truth.

When we arrived in California, we stayed at my grandpa and grandma's house. Apparently, when my dad was drunk, he would call my grandpa asking if we were there. On the other side of the country, he was furious that my mom left with me and Della. He would scream at my grandpa, "I'm going to come to the house and take my kids!" My mom was constantly worried that he would make good on his threat.

Within a few months, my mom reunited with a friend from high school named John and began a romantic relationship with him. To make sure my dad couldn't locate us, my mom wanted to find a new place to live. John had family living in Santa Ana, California. They thought that would be a good place to raise us and stay hidden from my dad. Mom, John, Della, and I eventually moved to Santa Ana when I was five years old. Compared to our former life of living on the sailboat, Santa Ana was a dream come true. I remember having a King Cobra Big Wheel that I rode around the apartment complex, meeting new friends. The weather was sunny and warm most of the year.

After living in Santa Ana for a few years, we moved to Tustin into a bigger apartment. My early childhood in Tustin was as normal as any other kid's. Kids my age played outside all day and returned home when the streetlights came on.

Mom and John signed me up for karate and Little League Baseball. My mom volunteered as the team mom and came to all of my games. John was very supportive of both my baseball playing and karate. He practiced with me to better my baseball skills, and he drove me to and from my karate lessons. John felt like a dad to me. Life was great!

Mom found steady work at Brooklyn Pizza. Later, it became the hangout spot for me and my elementary school-aged friends. We would barge in after school, and my mom would give us free pizza to eat and quarters to play the arcade games. My friends loved my mom. She never ran us out or made us feel like we were in the way. I remember experiencing real joy and laughter at that time in my life.

One day at the pizza place, I noticed an older guy with a gun in his pocket. I hadn't seen too many guns in my life and was curious.

"Did you see that?" I spoke under my breath to my friend, who was playing a video game.

"What?"

"That guy," I said, pointing as subtly as possible. "He just put a gun in his pocket."

As much as I was scared, I was also intrigued.

My mom and John started getting into some heated arguments. I woke up many times in the middle of the night with them screaming at each other. Mom cried a lot from these arguments and just seemed unhappy overall. We were in a vulnerable position because my mom didn't earn much money working at the pizza place, and she needed John's income to help provide for me and Della. Once again, she endured a dysfunctional living situation because she needed John to help pay the bills and put food on the table.

Even though we experienced times of despair, I still remember having a great relationship with my grandma. Sometimes we would go on vacation with her and my grandpa in their RV, which she called "Harvey, the RV."

One time, she took me and my cousin to a toy store. She told us to grab whatever we wanted. We couldn't believe our ears. We could have *anything*. Clearly, she was in a much better financial position than my mom and John.

While we were there, I kept waiting for her to say something like "Just kidding! Put everything back on the shelves." Fortunately, that didn't happen. My cousin and I loaded up the shopping cart with as much stuff as we could. We were in toy-heaven.

Even though my grandma could afford many things that

my mom couldn't, she provided more than just vacations and shopping sprees. When she was around, I felt a genuine sense of family. We spent many holidays at my grandma and grandpa's house with my aunties, uncles, and cousins. Grandma was the glue that held the family together. But, then, one day, my mom came home and told me and Della that our grandma was sick.

"Della. Jimmy. Sit down," she said. "I have some bad news to tell you."

"What's going on?" I was worried.

"Grandma's sick. She has leukemia."

I didn't know what leukemia was, but I knew it wasn't good. I felt a lump growing in my throat, but I held back the tears.

"Is she going to die?"

"The doctors will take good care of her." I could tell that she was avoiding my question. Mom looked at me and rubbed my back. She saw the grief and pain on my face. "It's gonna be okay, Jimmy."

I stayed in my room that night, thinking about my grandma. She meant everything to me. I couldn't bear the thought of her dying. To make matters worse, life at home was becoming more and more chaotic.

Mom's relationship with John was deteriorating. The arguments between them grew more intense and more frequent. John was becoming more and more aggressive.

He'd scream at the top of his lungs while plunging his fist through a wall. One time he got so mad he put his head through the wall. Seeing an adult smash his head through a wall was crazy. Mom then hung pictures over the holes so no one would know what happened.

Toward the end of one month, when the rent was due, Mom noticed some of her money was gone. It was from a hidden stash of cash that my grandma gave my mom to help her pay the rent. Mom suspected it was John who took the money, and she confronted him.

"Where's the money, John?" she asked franticly.

He shouted, "I didn't take the fucking money!"

"Don't lie to me. What'd you do with it?"

After several minutes of screaming and insults, John finally admitted he had taken the money. He took it to gamble at the horse track in an attempt to get more money, which never happened. Finally, mom couldn't take any more of his lying and the fighting. After another screaming match, their relationship ended abruptly, and Mom kicked John out. Even though I had begun to fear and dislike John, I was kind of sad to see him go. He was the only "father" I had known.

As the struggles surmounted at home, my grandma's condition continued to worsen. Mom began taking regular trips to Los Angeles to visit her in the hospital. Della and I were often left with the neighbors or with one of my mom's friends. With no one to take me to baseball or karate, I had to quit. Thankfully, I still played baseball and basketball with my friends in a cul-de-sac in our neighborhood. An older guy named Brandon, a big brother of sorts, often organized the games and played with us. He knew that we all would love to play on an actual baseball field, like a real team, so he decided to help us out. We called ourselves the California Angels.

After a few practices, Brandon asked us if we were ready to play against other teams in the area. Unfortunately, we needed some money to get a real team together. Because we were excited and motivated, we found as much spare change as we could. We gave the money to Brandon who bought us a bunch of used equipment—gloves, baseball pants, jerseys, bats, balls, and helmets. Though not everybody matched, we pieced together a team uniform. Finally, we felt like we were a real baseball team, even if we resembled The Bad News Bears.

Eventually, Brandon challenged one of the Tustin National Little League coaches to a scrimmage game. We were excited to play an organized Little League game against a real Little League team.

We ended up losing that game badly. My teammates blamed each other when we lost, and started physically fighting with each other. While shaking hands with the other team and saying the obligatory "good game," I balled up my fist and punched one of the opposing players in the face. After that, the Little League coaches banned our team from the baseball fields. That was the first and only game the California Angels ever played.

Unfortunately, this behavior was a precursor to more trouble that I would get into. I was in the sixth grade when my behavior changed dramatically. With everything going on at home including my grandma's illness, it was too difficult for me to concentrate and stay motivated to do my schoolwork. I was always getting in trouble for disrupting class, and my grades declined. I also started getting into fights at school. The administration thought it was better to suspend me as a punishment instead of considering why I was acting out. Because of this and the lack of support at home, I fell further and further behind academically. It was a negative cycle of me falling behind, acting out, punishment, and falling behind some more. Eventually, some of my friends told me they could not play with me anymore because their parents said that I was "bad."

I started roaming the streets and gravitating toward a new group of friends—the local gangsters. Many of these new friends hung out at the Sunset Liquor store and the surrounding apartment complexes. These were the well-known territories of a gang called the Duce Tray Crips.

It didn't take long before I started committing crimes with some older homeboys, like stealing things, breaking into cars, and fighting. I was desperate to fit in somewhere and these guys accepted me. I was compelled to belong so I did what they did to feel included and important.

At times, I hung out at a local laundromat. Here, I noticed an older man who worked there. He rode a moped to work and always parked it in front of the laundromat. I watched him start it a few times when he was leaving. It looked easy enough to start, so I decided that I would try to steal it. One morning, I waited in front of the laundromat for him to show up. After he arrived, I watched him walk to the back of the laundromat. I jumped on his moped and took off. I rode it around for a couple of days, having fun with it.

Days later, one of the older homeboys, who also hung out at Sunset Liquor, convinced me to help him steal some things from a house across the street from where I live. The worst part of this was that I knew the family I was about to rob. But, again, I wanted to fit in so I was willing to do what my homeboy wanted. The father's name was Mr. Holloway, and I went to school with his son. Mr. Holloway was a high-ranking Marine who worked at the nearby military base. He was an intimidating person with that typical stoic Marine look.

Still, this didn't stop me from doing what I was about to do. I walked with my homeboy across the street to Mr. Holloway's house while listening to my homeboy's instructions for what to do once I got inside.

When we got to the house, we looked around to see if anyone was watching us, and that's when my homeboy opened the bottom of the garage door. I quickly rolled underneath the door and made my way inside.

My adrenaline was pumping as I looked for stuff to steal, but it was so dark in the garage that I couldn't see. I was only in there for a few minutes when I heard the garage door opening behind me. I thought my homeboy was coming in, but when I turned around, I saw Mr. Holloway.

"Don't move!" he shouted. "Stay right there." Mr. Holloway was angry, and I stood there like a deer in headlights. He called the police and kept me trapped there until they showed up. I was arrested for the first time in my life, and I was charged with felony burglary.

My mom was called, and she hurried to Mr. Holloway's

home. I remember the look on her face. She stood there staring at me like she had lost all hope for me. The disappointment she exuded was hard to take. She was in disbelief that her son was arrested—arrested for a felony.

"What were you thinking?" she asked. "Why would you break into his place?"

All I could muster was, "I'm sorry, Mom," knowing that I broke her heart. She was overwhelmed trying to make ends meet and worrying about her sick mother. And, here I was, making things worse for her. I was a disappointment to her and myself.

Somehow the cops determined that I was the suspect who stole the moped. A description of what the thief looked like must have been making the rounds in the police department. I no longer had the moped because I had stashed it at a friend's house and sold it to him after I found out I was being investigated for stealing it. I was eventually charged with two additional counts—theft of the moped and selling stolen property. I entered the juvenile justice system when I was in sixth grade and just eleven years old. One felony and two misdemeanors were more than enough to prove to the parents who had steered their kids away from me that they were right. I pled guilty and was sentenced to a work program on the weekends and placed on probation for three years.

Unfortunately, that was not enough to keep me out of trouble. Instead, not knowing how to deal with my emotions, the desire to feel included, and the lack of supervision, got me into more trouble. Not long after my first arrest, I committed my first strong-armed robbery (i.e., a specific type of robbery that is committed with the use of force or intimidation that does not involve a weapon).

I was with friends at a 7-11 convenience store with a few arcade games. We didn't have money to play, so we watched other people play. That's when we noticed a kid pull a wad of cash out of his pocket to exchange for quarters. Our eyes lit up. We quickly put a plan together to rob him. When he left the arcade, we followed him around the corner of the store, beat him up, and took his money.

At school the next day, the police showed up and questioned me and my friends. Unbeknownst to us, the kid we robbed went to the same school as us and pointed us out to the cops. I was arrested again—this time charged with strong-armed robbery. I took a plea deal and served time in juvenile hall.

I felt like a little kid when I first walked into the unit in juvenile hall. All the other boys there looked much older and bigger than me. Some even had mustaches. I was scared but tried not to show it.

I got transferred to the Youth Guidance Center (YGC) and was placed in the girls' unit. There were two other boys in that unit with me. I was somewhat insulted to be put with the girls, but I knew it was safer there for me given how young I was and the amount of testosterone flying around the boys' unit.

Once I got released from juvenile hall two months later, my mom took me to the hospital to visit my grandma. I finally got to see her for the first time since she became sick.

When I walked into her room, I noticed she had lost her hair and had bruises all over her body. It was heartbreaking to see her in that condition—weak and unable to keep her eyes open. Yet, I thought she would recover and be home soon.

The last thing she said to me was, "Jimmy, please stay out of trouble."

I promised her I would. "I love you, Grandma, and can't wait 'til you come home." That was the last thing I ever said to her.

No one told me her days were numbered, and that we were actually there to say our last goodbyes. Unfortunately, soon after that visit, my grandma passed away on July 13th, 1988. I wanted to respect her last wishes, but I was emotionally bankrupt, and I didn't know quite how to get my life turned around.

My mom did all she knew to try to discipline me and get me on the right track. She whooped me, put soap in my mouth, made me stand with my nose against a wall, and sent me to my room for days at a time. None of that worked. It only made me angrier—more negative emotions that I didn't know how to process.

My grandma's death marked a monumental shift in our lives. Losing Grandma took a heavy toll on our whole family. The sense of togetherness with my extended family died with her.

Chapter 3

TROUBLE BREWING

Grandma's death brought a huge sense of grief to everyone in our family, and our large extended family fell apart quickly. Grandpa began selling off all my grandma's possessions. Mom and the rest of the family were shocked. He then ran off with the rest of her money to Henderson, Nevada, where he married some woman and completely cut ties with our family. My mom had no one to turn to for support.

Mom continued to find jobs to help us get by, but the pay was never enough to support her, Della, and myself. We had to rely on government assistance.

I was spending a lot of time with two of my good friends. They had an uncle named Barry— also known as B Nut, in the streets. He had just moved to California from Kansas City. I remember him saying that at one time he had taken a bullet when he jumped out in front of a gun to save his brother's life. I thought he was brave to take a bullet for his brother.

While I spent time with these friends, my mom and Barry met. He provided comfort and support to her when my grandmother had entered her final days. I don't think Mom planned to fall in love with him and surely she wasn't looking for a new boyfriend, but they ended up forming a significant relationship after spending more and more time together.

Once Barry moved in, he got comfortable quickly, and

his bad behavior began. My mom had a knack for falling in love with bad men. One afternoon I walked into the house, and he was sitting on the couch. A beer was in one hand, his feet were propped on the table, and he was watching television. When I crossed the room, I accidentally walked in front of the TV. He yelled at me, "Watch where you're walking, boy!" I hated when he called me "boy." When I ignored him, he got up and approached me.

"Did you hear what I said?"

I rolled my eyes. "Yeah, I heard you!"

He grabbed me by my shirt with his eyes looking like they were about to burst out of his head. I could feel his grip tightening around me as I struggled to get out from under him.

"Don't ever talk back to me, boy!" I felt and smelled his hot breath reeking of alcohol. He pushed me away and walked back to the living room.

I tried to stay out of our apartment as much as possible by hanging out with my friends. We loved playing ding-dong ditch. We'd ring someone's doorbell or knock on their door and then run to a good hiding place to watch them open the door to find nobody standing in front of them. We thought this prank was hilarious.

We often went to the same apartments because we liked seeing how frustrated some neighbors became when they were repeatedly pranked. The more we played this game, the more we rewrote the rules to make it more and more fun. Finally, we decided that whoever rang the doorbell had to hide as close as possible to the door without getting caught.

One night, we returned to an apartment where we had repeatedly pranked the man who lived there. It was my turn to knock. I pounded on the door as loud as I could and dashed to the nearby bushes, right next to the front door, waiting and watching for the people at home to answer.

My friends were hiding across the street and devising their own plan. They thought it would be funny to give up my hiding spot when someone opened the door. As soon as the angry man opened his door, they started yelling from across the street, "Hey! He's in the bushes! Look down to your left! He's the guy who banged on your door!"

Now the prank was on me.

The man at the door looked down in my direction. I jumped out of the bushes and jetted down the street as fast as possible. As I ran, I heard my friends across the street cracking up laughing. They eventually caught up to me, and we stood there laughing together.

"You guys got me good," I laughed. "I thought he was going to kick my ass!"

We passed the time another way by scaling into someone else's backyard when they were not home and jumping on their trampoline. We did get chased out of this backyard a couple of times as we were sometimes still there as the family arrived home. They were not too thrilled with a bunch of unknown kids playing in their backyard.

One day, we got bold and scaled the wall after we saw the family inside eating dinner. We went in for a quick jump, thinking they would run us off, but they didn't. I remember wondering what they were thinking, and I started to feel sad. Here we were, three pathetic kids without our own backyards and so desperate to have fun that we used other people's trampolines.

The three of us all felt that same jealousy and sorrow. "Fuck them!" One friend shouted. I joined in. "Yeah, fuck 'em. Let's get outta here." We laughed it off and left.

While most of my friends were having fun on the weekends, I had to endure a court-ordered work program. Every weekend in seventh and eighth grade, I woke up early and worked all day. The work usually consisted of picking up trash, pulling weeds, and cleaning other landscapes from sunrise to sunset. Sometimes, if we were lucky, we got to pick trash up on the beach.

The other kids and I were heavily supervised and graded each day on our work performance. Depending on our performance, we received a grade anywhere from an A to an F. If we received an F, we had to spend the night in juvenile hall. Some days, the supervisors would make us work extra hard, but none of the supervisors were as tough as Ivan—appropriately known as Ivan the Terrible. Whenever we had him as our supervisor, we knew we were in for a long, grueling day. At the beginning of each workday, he assigned us all Fs and said we had to work our way up beyond the F. He had no rhyme or reason for moving someone up or down the grading scale. It gave all of us a sense of helplessness and was demoralizing.

Ivan seemed to have it out for me and he picked on me more so than the others. He probably picked up on my shitty attitude. The work program kept me out of trouble during the time that I was there. I worked hard, sweating, digging, bagging up weeds, and picking up trash. Then I'd hear Ivan the Terrible shout, "Rumsey, you are at a D minus!" So, I would pick up the pace, trying not to spend the night in juvenile hall for the night.

One scorching, hot summer day, when the temperature was pushing triple digits, I showed up at the work program wearing a tank top. What I didn't realize was that tank tops violated the dress code. Ivan the Terrible spotted me walking up. He called someone over his radio and another county employee showed up.

He was there to book me into juvenile hall for the night. They didn't believe me when I said that I only wore the tank top because it was hot—that I was not intentionally violating the dress code that I didn't even know about. Too bad for me, I guess, as I had to spend the night in juvenile hall. I only had a few more days of the work program to complete after that day. Thankfully, I made it through to the end by keeping my head down, minding my own business, and not daring to upset Ivan the Terrible.

The next time I got arrested and went to court, the judge suggested that I participate in the work program as an alternative to being incarcerated. I declined the option, "I'm never doing that again. I'd rather be locked up."

When I wasn't in school or juvenile hall, I was usually out in the streets and up to no good. My mom did her best to buy me new clothes and shoes, but she couldn't afford the clothes and shoes that I wanted. I did not want to go to school with knockoff brands and get teased by my friends. We were all bullies when it came to making fun of each other and making other kids feel like shit for wearing knockoff brands.

My mom always bought me a brand of jeans where they had the policy to replace the jeans if a tear happened in the knee of the jeans—my mom was all over this. If I needed new jeans, she would rip the patch on the knees and return them for a new pair of jeans. Those pants and my Payless shoes got me laughed at so many times. Eventually, I got tired of it and started stealing the clothes and shoes I wanted. I would go to department stores and steal name-brand shoes. My method was to wear the cheap shoes that my mom bought me into the store, swap those out with the name-brand shoes, and walk out.

Getting away with minor crimes like this made me feel invincible, and I started to try my hand at stealing more expensive things like car stereos, money, cars, jewelry, and motorcycles. I even broke into a few homes. One of my partners in crime was my friend, JP. He was from Santa Ana and we went to the same school. When JP and I first met, we became friends right away. He was already legendary for stealing cars, and I was notorious for getting into all kinds of trouble. It didn't take long before we were stealing cars and committing crimes together. In eighth grade, we would steal cars and drive ourselves to school.

One of our first crimes together was stealing two cars in another county—a Toyota minivan and a Toyota MR2. We raced them on the freeway back to Orange County. After that, we'd use the minivan to steal miniature motorcycles to ride around the city.

A few days after stealing the minivan, there was a school dance at the junior high school from which I had recently been expelled. I wanted to go to the dance and see my old friends, so I went to where we had stashed the minivan, and to my surprise, it was still there. I hopped in, used a screwdriver to start it, and was on my way to the dance.

As I approached the school, I looked across the street and saw a police car driving in my direction. At thirteen years old, I could barely see over the steering wheel. As we slowly passed each other in the middle of the intersection, the cop sized me up. I knew that I looked guilty. It was clear to the officer that something didn't look right.

The cop turned his car around.

"Shit!" I yelled. Panicked, I took a quick right turn and punched the gas pedal to the floor. Once I got to the end of the street, I quickly took another right turn leading into an empty lot.

When I lost sight of the cop, I stopped the minivan, quickly jumped out of it, and leaped over a wall into an apartment complex. I ran through the complex and scaled another wall that took me to a riverbed. I followed the dry riverbed into the neighboring city of Santa Ana to my friend's house. Fortunately, I had gotten away from the cops but didn't get the chance to see my old friends at the school dance.

Days later, I was walking through the neighborhood, very close to where the cop had chased me. It was just my luck that the same officer was cruising down the street. Our eyes met and he recognized me. The officer hit his siren—*whoop, whoop.*

I took off again, running straight toward my friend's apartment. As I was running down the street, I saw my friend looking out his window. I shouted, "Open the door, open your door!" I was sprinting at full speed to his apartment with the cop right behind me.

My friend disappeared from the window and locked his door, so I couldn't get in. I was pissed but it was a smart move on his part. I pounded on the door with my fist, knowing he wouldn't let me in. Finally, the cop reached me, tackled me to the ground, cuffed me, and threw me into the back of his police car.

The cop questioned me about the stolen minivan. For whatever dumb reason, I easily confessed to being the driver. I sure wished my mom would have given me her advice sooner—"If you get into trouble and are questioned by the police, say nothing. Anything you say can and will be used against you."

I learned this lesson the hard way. My confession about the minivan was all they needed to charge me with grand theft auto. I was on my way back to juvenile hall.

This time, I was sentenced to serve seventy-five days in juvenile hall, be on house arrest when I was released, and have my probation extended for another three years.

After serving a few months in juvenile hall, I returned home on house arrest. Barry was becoming such a nightmare at home that I didn't want to be there at all but I didn't have any other choice with the monitor on my ankle. We didn't speak to each other unless we were arguing about something. He treated me like he hated me and he had frequent mood swings. It was getting hard to live under the same roof as him. And, quite frankly, I hated him too. After my house arrest ended, I spent as much time away from home as possible.

Chapter 4

BLINDSIDED

I couldn't believe Mom was still putting up with Barry. Maybe she didn't want to go without his income or maybe she didn't want to admit to another failed relationship. Sadly, she kept him around despite the carnage he brought into our lives.

Mom was working at a sandwich shop called Tummy Stuffers, and she got Barry a job there, too. I kept asking her to leave him, but she kept saying she needed him. The sandwich shop owners allowed Mom and Barry to rent one of their houses. When we moved in, it appeared to be an upgrade from our old place. But there was a huge problem with this house.

It had rats that lived in the gaps between the walls. We could hear them scurrying throughout the house and inside the walls at night. We were constantly setting traps to catch them. Every so often, I would get a horrible whiff of a dead rat stuck behind the walls.

What was even worse than living with the rats was living with Barry. When Barry wasn't working, he was at the house. I would find Brillo pads and car antennas underneath the couch which confirmed his drug use. When he'd put his hoodie over his head, I knew he was high and that I really needed to avoid him.

Drugs and alcohol weren't the only things Barry abused. He was extremely verbally abusive to my mom just about every day. Barry would belittle and insult her, calling her names. I hated hearing it. I was at my breaking point when Mom told me Barry's brother, Courtney, was coming to live with us. He was 25, ten years older than me, and his nickname was "Fats." He had just gotten out of a prison in Missouri.

When Courtney walked into our home, I felt my body tense up. Here was another Barry—I was sure that he was ready to make my life twice as hard as it already was. Instead, he immediately began cracking jokes.

"I'm not fat. I'm big-boned, motherfucker," he said as he walked in. Then he turned around, looking at the living room. "Oh man, I didn't know it would be this nice."

"Oh, please," my mom said, laughing. I stood in the hallway, watching. "Courtney, this is Jimmy."

Courtney walked over to me, extending his hand for me to shake. "Hey, little man, my name's Courtney."

"Hey," I said.

"We're gonna get into a lot of trouble together," he laughed, with my mom shaking her head.

"You better not," she groaned.

Barry looked annoyed, so I went back to my room. Maybe this Courtney joker would not be so bad after all. I didn't know then what Courtney would mean to me later.

It wasn't long before Barry started treating Courtney like he treated me. Barry would kick us both out of the house at the same time for no reason at all. As I got older, Courtney became like an uncle to me and would hang out with me and my homeboys.

At the house, Barry woke me in the very early morning

by banging on my bedroom wall, yelling, "Rumsey! Hurry up! Get your ass up and out of this house!" Barry would never call me by my first name. He always referred to me as Rumsey or "boy."

The first time Barry hit me was not a time I would ever forget. He and my mom were about to leave the house when Barry started ordering me to do chores. *Who is this guy trying to tell me what to do? He's not my father.*

It bothered me that my mom was allowing this asshole to have authority over me. A surge of anger overcame me and without thinking, I hocked a loogie into my mouth.

Barry glared at me with an evil look in his eyes, "Do it. I dare you." Without hesitation, I spit the loogie in Barry's face. Knowing I had crossed the line, I took off in fear and ran down the street as fast as I could. Barry couldn't catch me.

When my mom and Barry returned home, I was in my bedroom. I didn't know what to expect because Barry was so unpredictable. When he walked into my room, I noticed he was holding something in his hand. It was a wire from what looked like a window screen. He came after me with it.

I turned around to protect myself from getting hit in the face, and he started whipping me. He hit me several times with it while I tried to dodge the wire. The giant welts stayed on my back for a long time.

More than ever, I wanted him out of our lives. I would try to convince my mom to kick Barry out of our house and leave him. I thought our life would improve if Mom could cut ties with him. Frequently, I asked her why she was choosing Barry over me. I also started asking her more about my dad. I suspect that I was really missing a decent male figure in my life as I entered my teenage years. I had the illusion that he was more decent than my mom gave him credit for—afterall, he had to be better than Barry. Mom gave her usual answer, "He's dead or in prison." It was becoming clear that I'd never get the truth from her. She'd get annoyed when I asked about him. I thought that she must have really hated him because she never encouraged me to find him. In reality, she feared that if I found my dad, he would take me and Della away from her—something her heart couldn't handle.

I had an entirely different version of what would happen if I found my dad. I projected so much goodness onto him. He would be the person I wanted and not the person he most likely was. He would give me the support I needed, especially on how to deal with Barry. I wanted to reach out and talk to him. I wanted to call him up and say, "Hey, Dad. It's me, Jimmy! What should I do about Barry?"

With no one to turn to for support, I struggled to make it through most days. It was hard for me to stay out of trouble, and my anger issues just became more visible. It felt like no one was paying attention to me and I had no one to talk to about what I was going through. I just bottled it all up inside. I used to lie in bed at night and think, "When the hell does this end?" *Never* was always the answer.

It was too much for me to handle. I was losing hope and couldn't cope. I contemplated suicide as early as thirteen-years-old, thinking it was my only way out. I was also obsessed with thinking about ways to kill Barry.

His physical abuse toward me was becoming more frequent. When I was fourteen-years-old and my mom was at work, he stormed into my bedroom while I was lifting weights.

"Clean your room!" He yelled. When he left, I ignored his demand and continued lifting weights instead.

About ten minutes later, the door swung open and Barry barged in. As he came through the door, he looked different. I knew he was high on something. "You heard what the fuck I said!" He shouted with rage in his voice. His large frame blocked the entrance of my bedroom doorway. I had nowhere to go. I was trapped and terrified.

"You gonna fuckin' listen to me, boy! You think I'm playing with you?" He picked up one of my ten-pound weights, which was made of concrete and encased in a burgundy plastic shell. In one swift motion and without hesitation, Barry swung the weight and hit me right in the middle of my forehead.

It knocked me unconscious.

When I woke up, I was alone. I saw stars and my head pounded. I was trying to figure out how I ended up on the ground. Slowly, I remembered what had happened to me. If Barry could do that to me, what else would he do? I didn't want to take any chances. My instincts took over and I jumped out of my bedroom window, not wanting to encounter Barry again if I walked out of my bedroom door. I ran down the street as fast as I could.

I sprinted over to my neighbor's house. When I got there, I knocked on the front door. I was standing there crying, with a giant knot on my forehead.

They looked shocked. When I told them what had happened, they called the police. When the cops arrived, they checked my medical condition, called an ambulance, treated me, and took my statement. After that, Barry was handcuffed and arrested.

Barry told the officers that I was lying about the whole incident and downplayed all our problems at home. The story Barry told was that I tripped and landed face-first on the weight while working out. It was all just an accident. I couldn't believe my ears. He had just knocked me out cold and it was *my* fault. The police took Barry down to the station for further questioning. My mom left work and went to the police station to see what had happened.

I was lying on my bed when I heard the front door open. I thought it was my mom coming back from the police station. To my disgust, Barry's voice penetrated the silence. I panicked. My heart was racing, and my head was throbbing. I could not believe we were back in the same house together.

Angry, I went outside to confront my mom. She was on the porch smoking. "What's going on?" I asked in disbelief and anger. "How can you have this guy living here after what he did to me?"

"What did he do to you?" *What the fuck?! What the hell was happening just now?*

"You know what he did. I'm sick of this! I'm sick of

living here with that asshole."

"Watch your mouth, Jimmy," she said as I slammed the door behind me. *Yes, my mouth. That was the problem here.*

Barry had his head covered with a hoodie as I walked past. I was terrified of him and couldn't believe I had to share the same house with him. I was worried he might kill me. From then on, I would run away for days at a time, staying wherever I could lay my head.

If I didn't feel like I was unimportant before, I felt it now—my life didn't matter, even to my mom. I stopped caring—I became cold-blooded and violent. I took my anger out on people in the streets. I would spend the next ten years of my life doing drugs, drinking, fighting, stealing, robbing, shooting at people, and dodging bullets. I just didn't give a fuck.

Chapter 5

AFFILIATED

It all started innocently enough when the older homeboys offered me a sense of belonging and brotherhood. They considered me to be "affiliated," but I never claimed to be from the Duce Tray Crips until I was fourteen. As I got older, I started spending more time with friends that were gang-bangin'. It was more like I grew into that lifestyle rather than jumped into it. The homeboys gave me the nickname, "Slim," and made me feel like family. It felt good to be a part of something even if it meant engaging in more dangerous and reckless behavior.

At school, I was becoming a constant nuisance to my teachers. One time, when a teacher turned around to write on the chalkboard, I threw a crayon at him. For this, the principal paddled me three times with a wooden board.

Another time, I was misbehaving in some way and my mom had to come to sit in my classes with me. This did nothing to stop my bad behavior. In fact, I continued to mouth off so much to teachers that one became irate and grabbed me by my neck and choked me.

Because of all the fights and trouble that I was getting into at school, they expelled me from the Tustin Unified School District during my eighth-grade year and placed me at Summit, a school in the Santa Ana Unified School District. It was a small school in the back of a church. Although I didn't realize it then, I am quite certain it was a school for delinquent kids. When I arrived at Summit, I felt like it was a good fit because I knew some kids there from juvenile hall.

They knew me for being a class clown. One day in class, I disrupted the teacher's lesson by cracking jokes with a couple of other students and talking back to the teacher. The teacher didn't think what I said was funny, so he yelled at me and sent me to the office to be disciplined. As I walked down the hall to the principal's office, I was fuming after feeling like the teacher intentionally embarrassed me. I sat in the office ruminating in my own anger about how I could get back at that teacher.

With a few minutes to go before the end of the class period, I left the front office and returned to the classroom. While the other students were waiting for the bell to ring, I opened the door. Everyone turned around and looked at me. They looked surprised that I had returned. The teacher again ordered me to leave. He walked toward me when I didn't leave and shouted, "Get back to the office now!"

I glared back at him and responded defiantly, "Make me."

The teacher approached me as I stood by a bookshelf in the back of the classroom. I waited for him to get within arm's reach, then I snatched one of the hardback textbooks off the bookshelf. I swung the book at him and hit him in the face.

An uproar among the students across the classroom broke out. Everyone was in shock, especially the teacher. He started yelling and retreated to his desk to call for help.

The bell rang to end the class period, and I took off to my next class. When I got there, I acted as if nothing had happened. Of course, I knew my actions would have consequences.

When the next class was about to start, a teacher came and grabbed me out of the classroom. He escorted me back to the office. The administrator in the office had called the police, my mom, and my probation officer. When the cops arrived, I was arrested and charged with assault and battery. I was expelled from Summit and later sentenced to serve time at… you guessed it, juvenile hall. The court mentioned I had no respect for authority and no remorse. That was a pretty good assessment of me at that time.

They locked me up in juvenile hall so often that it felt like a second home to me. I even earned the nickname "F-U" from some of the staff who worked there because whenever they questioned me, I would usually reply, "Fuck you." Those two words were all they got out of me most of the time.

Upon my release, my new terms of probation included that I continue to attend the Youth Guidance Center's (YGC) day school program. Most of the youth who went to this school were incarcerated at the facility, but some high-risk kids, like me, were placed there by probation or the courts. There were about 30 of us that attended the YGC day program school. Allowing delinquent kids to hang out with other delinquent kids probably isn't the best recipe to get kids to change.

To get there each morning, I took the city bus from Tustin to the main bus terminal in Santa Ana. I then connected to another bus that would take me to a meeting spot with the other students. We got into county vans and were transported to YGC. Once we arrived at the facility, we walked in a single file line into the bathroom, five at a time, for a strip search. We were told by the YGC staff, "Take all your clothes off, turn around, lift your feet, squat, and cough." It was a humiliating experience to go through every day.

Somehow, I did well academically at the YGC day school and graduated from eighth grade there.

In the fall of 1990, I was allowed back into the Tustin Unified School District. My first year at high school was at Tustin High School. I was excited about being able to go back to school in Tustin so I could hang out with my friends. I joined the football team and played wide receiver and strong safety. It didn't take long before I was locked up again for stealing a car while on the team. It got to where my teammates had to explain to the coaches my whereabouts by telling them I was on vacation. Eventually, my coaches learned that "vacation" meant I was locked up.

My time at Tustin High School didn't last long. The next expulsion took place just a few months into my freshman year. One day, I was listening to my headphones in wood shop class and joking with a friend. It became clear to the teacher that I didn't care what he was saying. He walked up to me, grabbed my headphones, and locked them away in a locker.

I was in no mood to have my music taken away from me.

"What the hell? Give it back," I yelled at the teacher.

"Sit down," he said. "You can't listen to your music

when you're in class. So sit down, or I'm going to send you to the office." He said this as if it should have had some impact on me. Remember… I had no respect for authority.

"Give me my fucking headphones back," I shouted. All the kids in the class got quiet. They knew this was not going to end well.

"You can get them at the end of the day. Now sit down!" Again, he talked to me as if he thought he could scare me into submission.

I was not having it. "If you don't give them back, I'm going to blow this fucking room up," I screamed.

I was fuming, standing within a foot of the teacher. It was apparent I was making him nervous. He called the principal and told me to report to the office. I walked down and waited while the principal called my mom and my probation officer. When they showed up, we went over the whole incident, and they all agreed that Tustin High School was not a good fit for me.

They placed me at Hillview, a small continuation high school in Tustin. Some of my homeboys went there, and we had some rivals there too. One rival, in particular, Justin, had just moved from Santa Ana to Tustin. When I first met him, he was fresh out of a prison for youth known as a "gladiator school" because of all the violence there.

Justin and I crossed paths outside of a classroom during the passing period. Justin sized me up. "Where you from?"

"Duce Tray."

His eyes grew wide. He responded, "Shelley Street."

I immediately got into a defensive stance, ready for a

fight. Shelley Street was the name of a Santa Ana Blood gang. We exchanged some heated words and then noticed some teachers coming our way. We casually walked away from each other although still mad-dogging each other.

Our P.E. teacher, Mr. Turner, noticed my homeboys and I liked to play basketball during lunchtime. So one day, Mr. Turner came over and asked if we wanted to form a basketball team and compete against other schools. This sounded fun to us, so we agreed. He also asked Justin if he wanted to join the team and, surprisingly, he said yes.

Mr. Turner didn't realize that Justin and I were rivals and that my friends and I did not get along with him. However, we all wanted to play on a basketball team, so we gave it a shot. Mr. Turner created a basketball program at the school for us and, as surprising as it sounds, Justin and I formed a decent friendship because of our love for basketball.

One day, Mr. Turner pulled me aside and said, "Jimmy, leave whatever problems you have outside of the school out there. Do what you come to school to do and that's to learn." I respected Mr. Turner and what he had to say, but his influence was not enough to change me when I was outside of school.

Chapter 6

JUVIE DAYS

My troubles far superseded Mr. Turner's help. A month rarely passed when I didn't have a court date on my calendar. One night, I was joyriding with some friends. We were driving around in a stolen red 1992 Acura Integra, and before I knew it, the cops were behind us. They pulled us over and arrested all of us. It was the second time I was charged with grand theft auto.

It was February 1992, at the Superior Court, State of California of Orange County, when the district attorney and judge indicated I was to receive a sentence of six months. However, they told me if I pled guilty, they would lighten my sentence to only four months in my home away from home—juvenile hall.

I told the judge I was trying to get out of California and join the Job Corps, a government-run job training program. The judge agreed that if I got into the program, the courts would allow me to leave without having to spend more time in juvenile hall. However, the Job Corps rejected my application because of my criminal record, which included multiple felonies. When I returned to court later that month, I pled guilty, took the deal, and prepared to do some more time behind bars.

In 1992, I was once again booked into juvenile hall. By this time, I was sixteen and tired of being locked up. Every day was the same. I would work out by doing push-ups, sit-ups, and jumping jacks to pass the time. There were no toilets in the cells at juvenile hall. When I had to go to the bathroom, there was a button I pushed inside my cell to access the intercom. I would let the officer know if I had to take a "sit down or stand up." Then they'd unlock my door from the control center, and I would walk down the middle of the hall towards the bathrooms with my hands behind my back at all times. This was the procedure every single time I had to use the bathroom.

While serving my time, I often disobeyed the rules by disrespecting the staff or kicking and banging on my cell door until the staff came to restrain me. As a punishment, the staff would place me in a well-padded rubber room so I couldn't hurt myself. They would also make me hand-write the juvenile hall rules twenty-five times as a punishment. I was consistently breaking rules number nine and ten at the facility. Rule nine was, "Do not be disruptive (yelling, screaming, cursing, arguing, agitating others, teasing, or engaging in horseplay). Do not engage in any behavior that interferes with the peaceful, orderly atmosphere of the institution, or with any activity being carried on within the institution. Do not talk to staff members or other people in an unacceptable manner. Do not be disrespectful." And Rule number 10: "Follow directions – Do not refuse or fail to follow staff directions."

I was lucky to get transferred from the main juvenile hall center to another detention center. This place was more of a minimum-security detention facility. I liked it there. Not to mention, the food was better too.

When I arrived, they assigned a counselor to me and he

genuinely seemed like he wanted to help me. He hooked me up with a job working on the linen crew, where a few other inmates and I did laundry and put shower rolls together for the rest of the inmates. A shower roll consisted of a shirt, a pair of socks, underwear, a washcloth, and a towel. I received a paycheck every week, which I could spend at the commissary to buy snacks and drinks. During the day, we attended school and after school, we had time to go outside. I always looked forward to playing basketball.

I became friends with some of the other basketball players. I even became close with one of my teachers who liked to play basketball. His name was Mr. Anderson. He would sometimes get on the court and play with us. My counselor would sometimes play, too. After a couple of weeks of playing, we discussed having an inmate versus staff basketball game. It surprised us that Mr. Anderson and my counselor agreed to it and set up a date for us to play them.

I was looking forward to the day of the game because I thought we would beat the staff and all the inmates would love to see it. Everyone surrounded the court on game day to watch us play a five-on-five full-court game. This was when we learned just how good Mr. Anderson was at basketball. He put on quite a show, passing, scoring, and playing good defense. We gave it our all, but the staff ended up taking the win. The game we played against each other was memorable and eased the tension in the facility.

After I served my time again, I returned home. Predictably, I was soon back out on the streets and up to no good. My mom and Barry quit working at Tummy Stuffers, and the sandwich shop owners told us we had to move out of their rat-infested house. We ended up moving into a townhome with much better living conditions.

Mom and Barry were still fighting constantly and he was still making my life miserable. I repeatedly asked myself the same question — *Why did I have to roam the streets while he got to stay?* I kept thinking my life might improve if he wasn't around anymore.

Things got a little better as I got older and got a job. I worked at a sandwich shop and saved enough money to buy a blue scooter. I used that scooter to go to work, to find pickup basketball games around the city, and get away from home.

Eventually, I saved up enough money to buy my first car, a brown 1967 Buick LaSabre for five hundred bucks. I drove everywhere — the beach, Hollywood, Bristol Street, and Santa Ana. I even drove it to Las Vegas a few times with some friends. The amount of relief I felt in that car directly correlated to the distance I drove away from home.

Because it was a unique car, it was easily recognizable, especially to the cops who knew me. I was always looking over my shoulder for the Gang Unit led by Officer Jeff Blair, known as Pac-Man. His nickname came from the character played by Sean Penn in the 1988 movie *Colors*. Pac-Man was a hotheaded rookie cop learning the beat.

It seemed like every day I would see Pac-Man and his partners tailing me in my Buick. They'd pull me over all the time to search my car and rattle me as much as possible.

My homeboys and I would always meet up in front of my apartments. A three-foot high perimeter wall with iron fencing outlined the complex. We chilled there, drank, got high, and shot dice almost daily. The Gang Unit would often cruise by the apartments to scope us out.

I became good friends with MoMo. She lived directly across the street from me and had a younger sister and a younger brother named Frostee. MoMo and her family quickly became like family to a lot of us. While hanging out in front of the apartments, we would always see Frostee walking down the street with his football gear, heading home from football practice. Sometimes when we saw him coming, we would chase after him. Because Frostee was a running back, he often got away from us by sprinting through the apartments. When we caught him, we would tackle him to the ground and rough him up a little. There was no harm intended. He was like a little brother to us. We were having fun and trying to toughen him up.

As Frostee got older, some of us discussed jumping him into Duce Tray, but it was just talk. Occasionally, Frostee would make his way across the street and try to hang out with us. There was a time when I let him hit the weed we were smoking, but I usually told him, "Get out of here, Frostee. Get back across the street and stick with football." All the homies could tell that football was his primary focus. We wanted to see him succeed at it. When Frostee got older and into high school, he became a standout player and made a name for himself throughout the state. When I could, I went to his games to watch him play.

During this time, my mom got engaged to Barry. I shook my head in disbelief when she casually told me they were getting married. "You're crazy," I said.

"Don't be like that, Jimmy. He's going to be better."

"Do you actually believe the shit you are saying? It's nothing but lies you're telling yourself. He belittles you every day, Mom. He's going to end up killing you."

"Stop it," she said, half sad and half exhausted. It broke me to see her once again choosing this man over me, over her mental and physical health, and just over any chance of her life getting better. The thought of killing Barry came back to me. I never forgot about him whipping me with the wire cord and knocking me out with the weight. I wanted revenge for all he had done to me and my mom. Sometimes Barry would say to me, "Rumsey, I know when you get older, you're going to try to kill me." After an episode where Barry beat me up and kicked me out of the house, something snapped in my head. I was tired of taking his abuse and it was time to fight back. He was much bigger than me, but I felt like I had to do something.

I was sitting in my room listening to Barry berate my mom again.

"You're so fucking stupid, dumb shit!" he yelled. "You never fucking listen."

"Stop it," she said, scared.

"Shut the fuck up. Get the fuck out of my way, fat ass."

I could feel the heat rising in my body as I heard my mom cry.

She told him that she no longer wanted him there and he

48

needed to leave.

"I'm not going anywhere," Barry yelled. I heard a glass shatter against the wall.

"Stop it!" Mom pleaded.

"No one's gonna want you after me, bitch. You think anyone's gonna want a stupid ass like you?"

"Just go!" Mom sounded panicked. I'd had enough. I ran out into the living room.

"What the fuck is going on?" I yelled. "You heard her. It's time to leave!"

Barry came at me and started punching me. Mom screamed for us to stop, but the adrenaline had taken over. Finally, after we both landed several blows, Barry yelled at me, "Get the fuck out!" But he was the one who my mom wanted to leave, or so I thought.

Mom stormed out of the house, just frustrated with both Barry and myself. I called some of my older homeboys and asked them to come over to help me beat Barry's ass. I was waiting outside for them when they showed up, but Barry knew we were coming for him. He locked all the doors, barricaded himself in the house, and called 911.

The police arrived and detained us. The cops sat us on the curb for questioning. Once Barry saw the police, he stormed out of the house.

"These little punks trying to fuck with me. Now look at you. Rumsey, you wanna be like these guys? You ain't shit!" Barry continued taunting us, calling us names, knowing he was safe since the cops were there to protect him. When the cops questioned us, the look on Barry's face told me I'd have to sleep with one eye open from now on.

Barry knew there would be consequences for him for disrespecting the homeboys. No one got arrested and the cops made us go our separate ways.

Ironically, my mom and Barry caught me smoking weed when I was fifteen. After they yelled at me about it, Barry pulled me aside and asked me how much I paid for an ounce. From that moment on, I picked up weed for him and my mom. A few weeks after our last encounter, Barry drove me to my supplier in Santa Ana. When I went into the alley, I saw some of my homeboys there. These were the same homeboys that Barry was mouthing off to just a few short weeks ago. When they asked who I was with, I told them I was with Barry.

"Where is he?"

I replied he was out front in the car. They started walking that way. I tried to persuade them to let it go. I wasn't in the mood for another altercation with him. But, they didn't care. They went out to the street to confront him.

When they got to Barry's car, the homies said, "What's up, B Nut? What was that you were saying the other day?" I knew my homies had guns, and I thought they might kill him. A part of me hoped that they would.

Instead of Barry trying to act tough, he apologized. Even though I wanted Barry dead, I kept telling the homies, "It's all good. Don't trip." They left him alone, but not without leaving him with some parting words, "Don't put your hands on Slim ever again."

While driving home, Barry and I didn't say a word to

each other. I wondered if what happened was going to change things between us. *Would Barry stop messing with me out of fear of the homies retaliating?* While I was somewhat hopeful, I couldn't be sure. I mean clearly Barry didn't make decisions based on logic.

I made a small amount of money for hooking Barry up with the weed while also getting some for myself. I headed out front to smoke with some of my homies. As usual, we saw Frostee walking home in his football gear. This time, we didn't run after him. We walked across the street and talked to him about his upcoming playoff game, which he was excited to tell us about. I told him I would be there to watch him play.

I made it to the game and really enjoyed seeing him perform at such a high level. He was really good. And, I could tell he liked having me there. It also allowed me to escape the troubles in my life, even if it was just for a moment. In some odd way, listening to Frostee talk about his football dreams and how passionate he was about it gave me hope that my own future could be better one day.

Chapter 7

FIRSTBORN

I officially dropped out of high school in 1994. I quit the sandwich place and got hired at the new Popeye's Chicken restaurant that popped up in Tustin. When they first opened, it seemed like just about everyone in the neighborhood was getting a job there. I worked there with Justin, MoMo, and a few other people I knew from Tustin.

After work, I would hang out with Justin and some of our mutual friends in the alley on Alliance Street. We would hang out and drink there. I usually had extra cash because I started exchanging counterfeit money for real money. My method was to take counterfeit $100 bills, use them to buy the cheapest thing I could, and get the real money back in change. I did this at a few places where I had friends working at the cash register.

When I was about to turn 18, I met a girl that I liked. We started talking, but shortly thereafter, I was locked up again—this time for the possession of a deadly weapon. She and I were able to continue talking while I was incarcerated. This girl had a friend named Tasha who lived next door to her. Tasha had her own phone line in her bedroom. Whenever I called Tasha, she would run next door and bring the girl back to her house so I could talk to her.

Once I got out of jail, I was hanging out with Justin and some other friends, drinking and smoking. Being the cool person I thought I was, I carried a pager. One night, I received a page. When I called the number, it was the girl that I liked. She asked me for a ride home from a party that she was at. I asked Justin if he wanted to roll with me to pick up some girls. He decided to tag along.

When we arrived at the party, we picked up the girl and her friend, Tasha. The four of us drove back to Tustin, where I dropped them off at the Marine base. Before they got out of the car, we made plans to hang out the next day.

The following evening, while hanging out with my friend, Sean, I got a page from Tasha asking if I was ready to hangout again. Sean and I got in my car and headed to the Marine base to pick up the girls.

When we got there, Tasha was by herself. She said her friend couldn't come out with us. She jumped in the car and the three of us drove around, smoking weed and listening to music. At the end of the night, I dropped Tasha off at the base and took Sean back to his house.

Later that night, I received a page from Tasha. When I called her back, she asked why I had brought Sean.

I got the hint that Tasha wanted to be alone with me. She asked me to come back and pick her up after midnight. She was going to sneak out of her house and said to meet her near the wall at the corner of the base.

Around midnight, I drove back to the industrial parking lot outside the corner of the base, where Tasha told me to meet her, and waited for a few minutes. Then I saw Tasha making her way over the barbed-wire fence where a spot had been smashed down by people climbing over it. After she scaled the fence, she got into my car and we took off for a night out on the town. We drove around the city, getting to know each other and flirting—that other girl no longer held my interest.

While cruising, Tasha asked to drive my car, which was a bold request because I didn't let anyone drive my car. But instead of saying no, I told her that she had to sit on my lap if she wanted to drive. Without hesitation, she hopped onto my lap and took over the wheel. We were laughing and having a good time. As she was driving us around the city, I invited her back to my home.

Tasha agreed and we headed toward my place. When we got there, we quietly entered the house and I got Tasha situated in the living room with the TV on. I went into the kitchen to make a frozen pizza and some cherry Kool-Aid.

I was taking a huge risk being in the house with Tasha given that Barry was home. It would get ugly if he woke up and saw us there. I was prepared to run Tasha out of the house if I heard anyone coming from upstairs. We were quiet and hoped that Barry didn't smell the pizza in the oven. I went upstairs to peek into their room. Both were sound asleep with the fan blowing loudly. I pulled the door shut and considered the coast clear.

Tasha and I sat on the couch together, watching and laughing at *The Three Stooges*. We enjoyed the same humor, and I could feel the chemistry between us. I got closer to her on the couch and went in for a kiss. She didn't retreat but instead kissed me back. I asked her if she wanted to go up to my room. She hesitated at first but finally said yes.

After that night, Tasha and I would hang out every day. We had a routine. Tasha would skip school during the day or sneak out of her house at night to meet up with me.

It didn't take long before our relationship became serious. Tasha was cheerful and full of life, and I loved being in her company. She liked to crack jokes and we laughed a lot together. She brought light into my dark world.

We were both young and having fun, and within a few months, we received news that would change our lives forever. We went from hanging out, drinking, smoking, and enjoying each other's company to discovering that we were going to have a baby. My initial reaction was straight denial. I ignored Tasha and tried to push her away.

Rumors were swirling around our circle of friends so much that even my mom asked me, "Jimmy, did you get somebody pregnant?" I denied it, even though, deep down, I was certain the baby was mine.

I was nowhere near ready for the responsibility of being a father, so I publicly kept denying it. While Tasha was pregnant, she would call me and try to convince me that I was the father. "This is *your* baby, Jimmy."

I kept telling her, "Tasha, it's not my baby." But I knew — *how could the baby not have been mine?* We were together all the time.

Tasha was struggling over what to do about her pregnancy. She kept it a secret from everyone in her family, especially her father. Not knowing what to do, Tasha confided in her older sister, Tanya, and one of her friends. Tanya used that information to blackmail Tasha into doing her chores for her.

Tasha knew there was no way she could keep the

pregnancy a secret forever, so she wrote a three-page letter to her dad. Tasha handed the letter to him when he came home from work and then went to her room to await a response.

When she saw him next, his eyes were red and a look of extreme disappointment could be seen on his face. It didn't make matters any better when Tanya shouted, "And it's by a white boy!"

He didn't say much to Tasha for the next few days. Initially, he wanted Tasha to have an abortion. As he considered Tasha's other options, he enrolled her in a school for pregnant teens. He sought advice from a counselor and a teacher at the school and shifted his views about Tasha having the baby. Ultimately, he told her he would support any decision she wanted to make.

Tasha decided to keep the baby.

Over the next few months, we drifted even further apart. I cut off all communication with her.

I spent most of Tasha's pregnancy running the streets and spending time in jail. I seemed to always be running from something—from Barry, from my emotions, from the cops, and from my responsibilities. I took my anger out on other people in the streets. I also started experimenting with cocaine and PCP.

After getting out of jail for the umpteenth time, I knew I couldn't run away from my responsibilities much longer. I had to face the truth, so I called Tasha late one evening and asked her if I could come over.

"Yes, of course, Jimmy," she said. "I've been waiting to

talk to you."

From where I lived, I could walk to her house. I started in that direction and hopped over the barbed-wire fence onto the Marine base. Tasha snuck me in through the garage when I arrived at her home. We crept up the stairs to her bedroom, ensuring not to wake anyone. This was probably a bit of a bold move given that I was sneaking onto a Marine base and into the home of a Marine, but my mind was so warped I didn't think logically much of the time.

We both knew why I was there. Tasha was seven months pregnant with our baby. We needed to figure out how we should move forward with a baby on the way. As we were lying next to each other in her bed, we were listening to music, and then from out of the speakers, "Forever my Lady" by Jodeci started playing. We listened to the song's lyrics. They were prophetic.

> "So you're having my baby
> And it means so much to me
> There's nothing more precious
> Than to raise a family
> If there's any doubt in your mind
> You can count on me
> I'll never let you down"

Tasha and I paused in silence, looking at one another.

"Are you ready to be a dad, Jimmy?" Tasha asked.

I looked into her eyes, then looked away. "I gotta go," I said. Tasha looked shocked as I picked up my stuff and headed out the door. I left the house and wouldn't speak to Tasha again until after our baby was born.

I received a call on December 19th, 1994, around 9 p.m. It was Tasha's best friend. She informed me that our daughter was born. I felt my heart race. The news hit me like a ton of bricks. I didn't say a word. I just hung up the phone. *Click.*

The reality of being a father finally sunk in. Even though I did not see Tasha and the baby, I celebrated the birth of my daughter by hanging out with my friends.

At midnight, we walked up the street to the liquor store where one of my homies, Lil Ron, could legally purchase alcohol. He bought us all beer, and we returned to the front of the apartments to celebrate into the early morning. We made plans to meet up the next day.

Later that evening, Lil Smoke, Lil Ron, Rabbit, and a few other homeboys met me in front of my apartment, and we continued the celebration.

We were all having a good time that night when I noticed an older model Lincoln cruising slowly up the street. The car pulled off to the right and parked in front of MoMo's and Frostee's apartment.

The front of the car was facing us. Then the headlights went off. I didn't take my eyes off that car. I had an intuition that something was about to happen. When the traffic died down, I saw the Lincoln slowly creeping toward us with the headlights still off.

When the car got closer, I noticed a person on the passenger side sitting on the window ledge, hunched over the top of the car. This moment seemed to play out in slow motion. Shots from a gun that was aimed at us rang out.

I took cover behind a short brick wall and hit the ground. All I could hear were loud bangs and bullets whizzing over my head. The gun blasts were getting closer and closer. They were so close that I thought the car had stopped right in front of us. I didn't know whether I should stay put or get up and run. Once the shooter fired off all his rounds, the Lincoln peeled out and sped off into the night.

I knew the police would arrive soon to investigate. Everyone who was there at the scene scattered. I retreated into my apartment with a plan to act as if I'd been inside the whole time. In the gang lifestyle, talking to the cops is not something one did even if you weren't involved in the crime they were asking about. Doing so could get you killed.

The cops knew where to find me since it happened right in front of my apartment. They were soon knocking on my front door to question me.

"Did you hear or see anything, Jimmy?"

"No. I've been in the house, listening to music," I responded. "What happened?"

The cops knew I was lying. Afterall, gun shots were just fired outside of my apartment and there is no way I couldn't have heard that. But, that's all the information they would get from me. I laid low for the rest of the night as the police continued their investigation.

As I laid in my bed that night, I knew I could have been wounded and maybe even killed not even 24 hours after my daughter had been born. I thought about Tasha and our new baby. I heard that Tasha named her Shalah. I thought about my life and my future. I remember wondering, *"What am I supposed to do?"*

In the early morning hours, I received some clarity. I didn't want my child to grow up without a father like I did. So, I told myself I would be there for my baby no matter what. I faced an even more critical question, *"Could I even be a good father?"*

Of all people, Barry said to me, "Boy, that's your baby. You need to do the right thing and go see her!" This was after my mom and Barry had gone to see Shalah for the first time. They brought Shalah gifts and diapers. Tasha later told me that Barry held Shalah. I was shocked. I had never seen a soft side of him in my life. My mom and Barry knew that was my child.

My heart was in two different places. I continued my criminal way of life but a part of me also wanted to change and be involved in my child's life in a positive way.

I picked up the phone. "Tasha?"

She answered, "Hi, Jimmy. What's up?"

"Can I come over?"

"Yes, Jimmy, you can come over."

With my driver's license suspended, I rode my bike to Tasha's house. She snuck me in through the garage door, given I had yet to meet her parents.

I was nervous when I got to the room where our baby was. I did not know what to expect or how I would react. I turned the corner and walked into the room.

And there she was. Shalah. My daughter was asleep in her crib. I picked her up and cradled her in my arms. I didn't want to put her down or ever leave her side. She was so beautiful.

Shalah opened her eyes and stared at me. She had big, blue, beautiful eyes. After I saw her, I would never again deny that she was my child.

Standing in Tasha's bedroom that night holding our baby, I looked at Tasha and asked her if she wanted to start over and try again. Tasha nodded yes. She wanted to be with me. She wanted us to be a family.

This was the most mature decision I had ever made — to be a father to my child.

That decision was also a turning point in my relationship with Tasha. After that, we were together just about every day once again. I became addicted to the feeling I got being around Tasha and Shalah. I knew Tasha loved me because she couldn't hide that love. She always told me she had seen the good in me since we first met. Tasha always said, "I see the real you, Jimmy. You have a good heart. You're a protector, loyal and giving."

Because Tasha and I were getting serious about our relationship and trying to be a family, she wanted me to meet her family. I avoided meeting her parents for as long as possible because I didn't believe that they would think that I was good enough for their daughter. Afterall, I didn't even think I was good enough for Tasha.

After her dad found out we were together, he asked Tasha when he was going to meet me. Tasha set up times for us to meet on a few occasions, but I kept backing out at the last minute with some poor excuses.

"I can't come, Tasha. I hurt my back."

"I'd love to meet your family, but I'm busy."

It was clear I wasn't ready. For all I knew, her dad could have been another Barry. Then, after many attempts, Tasha called me and said, "Jimmy, when are you going to meet my family? My dad wants to meet you. It's time that you two meet."

"Okay," I knew that she was right. "When's a good time?"

"My dad said you should come over for family movie night on Friday, and you can meet everyone then."

The plan was set. Even though I sounded confident on the phone with Tasha, I was nervous. So many things were running through my mind, and I was stressed. I did not know what to expect.

First, I wasn't used to families doing things together. When Tasha said it was family movie night, I didn't even know what a "family movie night" meant.

Second, I was hesitant to meet her family because her father was a Marine. That was intimidating for me. I thought Tasha's dad would lecture and interrogate me about my schooling and work. I had no plans for my future. Deep down, I had nothing good to say about myself. I was ashamed of my background and ashamed of who I was.

When heading to family movie night, these thoughts were swirling in my head. Tasha called ahead and added me as a guest to enter the Marine base. For the first time, I checked in at the front gate. I received a pass from the guard and drove toward their house. It was a completely different experience from how I snuck onto the base the other times I had gone to Tasha's house.

As I got to her house and stepped out of my car, I prepared to make my best first impression. I told myself that even if they didn't like me, I would still be there for my child. I walked a little slower up to her front door than my usual pace and rang the doorbell, not knowing what to expect.

Almost immediately, Tasha swung the door open and greeted me with a big smile. She led me down the short hallway toward the living room. As I rounded the corner, Tasha's father was sitting on the couch.

"Hi, I'm Jimmy," I said.

Tasha's dad stood up, walked across the room, and shook my hand with a smile on his face. "Nice to finally meet you, Jimmy. I'm Sherman."

"Nice to meet you, Mr. Patterson."

To my surprise, he was easy to talk to, and I started to feel more comfortable in their house. Then the rest of the family came into the living room—Tasha's three sisters and her mom.

"This is Tanya, Monique, Shanise, and my mom," Tasha said. They all said hello but seemed skeptical of me. I realized it would be harder getting on the good side of the women in Tasha's family than it would be with her dad.

Everyone sat on the couch and we started watching *Die Hard.* It was one of the weirdest experiences I had ever had—siblings and parents getting along, enjoying each other's company, laughing while watching a movie, and eating pizza seemed so surreal.

I felt at peace. I felt welcomed into Tasha's family home. I expected Tasha's home life to be more like mine—chaotic, dysfunctional, unpredictable, and conflictual. But it wasn't. It was the complete opposite. They actually seemed to enjoy being with each other. It comforted me that my baby came from a loving family. When I got home later that night, I took it all in, sitting on my bed, just thinking. I was in a daze.

You could feel the love they had for one another. I knew at that moment I wanted a family like this for myself. Mr. Patterson welcomed me into their family and opened his home to me. Tasha's home would become my safe haven where I would visit Tasha and Shalah regularly.

Chapter 8

TEFLON

Y ou never knew what you were going to get with Barry. Sometimes, he felt disrespected if you said hello to him. Other times, if you didn't say hello to him, he would call you out for not speaking to him and say that you were being disrespectful.

When Tasha came to my house one day, she tried to avoid Barry because she never knew what kind of mood he was going to be in. Della opened the front door to let Tasha in. Barry was sitting on the couch watching TV. Tasha avoided him and nervously headed up the stairs. Barry didn't look or say anything to her. When she got halfway up the stairs, he yelled, "Okay, don't say hello, bitch!"

Tasha was scared, ran into my room, and told me what had happened. Barry told my mom that Tasha had to go. My mom came into my room and said to us that Tasha had to leave and that she would give her a ride home. After they left, I approached Barry, who was still sitting on the couch, "What's your problem? Why did you call Tasha a bitch?"

"Because she is a bitch."

He was such a fucking dick. We shouted at each other and things escalated quickly. Barry got up and came at me. I grabbed the first sharp thing I saw—a pair of scissors. I went after him. He ran out of the house through the back door, with me chasing him down the street.

While running, he turned around and taunted me. "Rumsey, you're in love!"

I quickly realized I wasn't going to catch him, so I turned around and went home.

While I was sitting at home waiting for him to come back, Mom returned from dropping Tasha off. Then the phone rang. Barry called Mom from a pay phone to tell her about the fight. He told her I chased him up the street with scissors. She came into my room. I knew what was coming.

"Jimmy, you shouldn't have done that. Now, he's all upset and doesn't feel safe with you here anymore. I think it's time for you to go."

I wouldn't say that he was wrong because I still wished he was dead. I would have killed him or had him killed if I knew for sure that my mom and Della wouldn't have then been homeless. I rolled my eyes. "You know what, Mom... Fine. I'm done with this. If you want to be with this asshole, then stay with him. Don't expect me to be in your life, too."

I called Tasha to tell her what had just happened. She and her mom came to pick me up right away. I then told Tasha's family about what happened and what life had been like with Barry. They now understood how bad things were for me at home. I think Mr. and Mrs. Patterson felt sorry for me knowing that my life at home was rough.

Although they didn't know the extent of my gang involvement, Mr. and Mrs. Patterson knew that I was not always innocent either. Still, they always saw the good in me and wanted me to be around for their daughter and granddaughter. I think Mr. Patterson knew that I could be something better than I was. He was a role model and father figure to me. His unconditional acceptance had a major impact on my life.

Given how good the Pattersons were to me, I didn't want the skeletons in my closet to catch up with me at their home and risk the safety of everyone else living there. Unfortunately, my fears would be realized.

After the altercation with Barry, I stayed with the Pattersons for a few days and then moved back in with my mom and Barry. The door to their apartment seemed like a revolving door with me moving in and out so many times. I sometimes wondered why they let me back in but our "family" was so dysfunctional and Barry did so many drugs, there was no making sense of it.

One night, my homeboys and I crossed paths with a guy in the streets. He told us he was with one gang and then with another. When one of my homeboys was tired of his lying, we beat him up.

The next day, I got a page from Tasha.

"911," it read.

I called Tasha right away and asked her what was up. She told me that some guy came by the house with his friends and warned her mom, "Tell your daughter that her baby daddy got something coming for him." One of my worst fears was coming true—my gang life and my life with Tasha were starting to intersect and it was happening at her house.

Tasha was scared. "Jimmy, the guys are still hanging out by my house. I don't know what to do."

The guy that we had beaten up the night before was the guy who delivered the message to Mrs. Patterson. He had known who I was and that Tasha had a kid with me.

After I hung up the phone with Tasha, I gathered some of my homeboys and we headed toward Tasha's place. As I pulled onto the base, I noticed that the car ahead of me had a sticker on the windshield that told the gate guards to let this car through without stopping it for questioning. With the gates open, the guards allowed me to slip through right behind that car. We drove towards the area where Tasha said the guys were hanging out. We spotted the group of guys in the street, and I saw the guy we had beaten up.

We pulled up to them and got out of the car. Most of the guys standing there ran, including the one we had beaten up. We confronted the ones who stayed, beat them up, and left a message for the guy who delivered the threat to Mrs. Patterson—he had something coming the next time we saw him. Afterward, we hurried to the cars to get off the military base as fast as we could.

Tasha's family did not like the drama, and they questioned Tasha about it. She downplayed it and said it wasn't my fault. She blamed the other guys for what happened. The military police investigated and intended to ban me from the base. Fortunately for me, they messed up and banned another friend of mine with the same name.

I had always tried to keep Tasha in the dark about my troubles, but it ended up on her doorstep this time. She didn't know how deeply involved I was. I didn't want her to worry about me, and the less she knew the better off she was. She could always claim that she didn't know something if she was ever questioned about anything that I did. She already knew more than I wanted her to know because the streets were always talking.

A few days after that incident on the Marine base, I was hanging out with some friends named Harold and Tony. We always had a good time hanging out, cracking jokes, and making each other laugh. Harold and Tony weren't from Duce Tray and wouldn't hang out with me at any one time for too long. They both knew when to part ways when things got serious. They usually had a keen sense of avoiding trouble, but not on this day.

We hopped in my '67 Buick and cruised around the block. As we pulled up to the light, The Circle K store was on the right. I looked over and saw some rivals from another gang hanging out in the parking lot.

While in broad daylight, I threw my car into park in the middle of the main street. Even though Tony and Harold weren't from my gang, I told them to come with me, "Come on, let's go smash these fools." We all exited the car, and the rivals fled into an alley on the side of the store. We had them cornered, or so we thought.

As we came closer, one guy turned around and pulled out a gun. He took a knee, aimed his gun at us, and started shooting. I don't know what I was thinking when I decided to run up on them without a gun, especially since they were known shooters and we had shootouts with them before.

We sprinted back to the car that was idling in the middle of a busy intersection. As I ran full speed toward my car to take cover, I could hear the loud gunshots being fired from behind me. I was hoping not to get shot in the back.

I got back behind the wheel of my car without getting shot. As I waited for Tony and Harold to get back in the car, the bullets kept flying in our direction. I hunched down to the side of the steering wheel, trying to take cover.

When Tony finally got to the car, he jumped in the back seat and took cover just as Harold slid into the passenger seat.

Harold yelled, "I'm hit!" I punched the gas pedal and sped away, keeping my head low to avoid bullets from hitting me. My adrenaline was pumping.

Once we got around the corner, Tony shouted, "He's bleeding in his back!" I looked over to check on Harold and saw blood all over his shirt and my seat.

"Sit up, Harold," I said, "Let me see your back."

He shifted over so I could look. The bullet struck him in his right shoulder. He was losing blood fast.

"I'm getting dizzy, Slim. I need help."

"Slim, hurry!" Tony shouted. "We need to get him to the hospital now!"

It all happened so quickly. I made my way through the streets toward the hospital. Luckily, it was close by, less than five minutes from where we were. When I pulled into the emergency room drop-off entrance, I told Harold and Tony to get out.

Once they did, I took off. I felt terrible for leaving them, but I didn't want to be questioned by the cops. So, I headed to where some of my homeboys were hanging out to let them know what had just happened.

When I got there, I told them that some rivals were

shooting at me, that Harold got shot, and that he was in the hospital. I knew the police would look for me after the description of my car got out. I had safely returned to my side of town when the police caught up with me.

Pac-Man showed up with his partner at my doorstep to ask questions. "Jimmy, what happened today at Circle K? There was a shooting. We know you were involved. Tell us what you know."

I told them that I knew nothing, "I was just cruising around with my music blasting. If there was any shooting, I didn't hear it."

Pac-Man and his partner knew I was lying. "Jimmy, we know you were there. Tell me, how did Harold get to the hospital?"

"I do not know what you're talking about." I refused to answer any questions.

Pac-Man said, "We already have enough information from Harold and Tony. Your friend, Harold, is lucky to be alive."

The next day I read the headline in *The Orange County Register*— "Tustin Police Seek Suspected Gunman." The article reported, "The shooting comes about a month after a stabbing involving members of the same gangs."

Because I was easily recognizable and had been shot at a few times in my Buick, my car was well-known, not only to the cops but also to my rivals. It was time for a new ride. I got rid of my 1967 Buick and bought a 1982 baby blue Monte Carlo.

I used this new car to pull off some robberies to get extra

cash. I was desperate for money and grabbed a couple of my homies to rob one of my drug connections. This connection always met me in the alley to do our transactions. He didn't know I had been watching him the last few times I picked up to see what apartment he hid his drugs in. This time, when we pulled up, we weren't there to pick up.

We parked in the alley, got our guns ready, and busted through the front door of the apartment. At gunpoint, we demanded everyone lay down on the floor as we ransacked the apartment. We made off with a lot of drugs and cash. That robbery went so well that I got a different group of homies together a few weeks later and returned to the same dope house to rob them again. I didn't tell my homies that this was the same spot I had robbed a few weeks prior. They probably would have thought it was a dangerous move to rob it again.

This time, we caught a guy near the apartment entrance and used him to make our way inside. One of my homies had a shotgun and I had a pistol. This time, as soon as we came through the front door with our guns drawn, some people inside started running out the back door.

We grabbed the ones we could and forced them to the floor at gunpoint. One of them started screaming, so I began to pistol-whip him in the back of his head a few times to shut him up. We knew we had to hurry and get out of there because he had screamed so loud and some others had run out of the apartment. We feared that the cops would be on their way soon.

We took what we could and quickly exited. When we got to the car to leave, the few people that had run out of the apartment were waiting for us by my car. I pointed my gun at them and yelled for them to back up. They didn't budge. One of my homies cocked his shotgun to shake them up. That was enough to make them run off.

Word on the streets spread about some crimes in which I was allegedly involved. Police started pulling me over everywhere I went, which made me assume that the police had informants feeding them information. The police constantly stopped me for traffic violations and probation searches.

Most traffic stops resulted in small traffic citations or arrests for petty crimes. More than anything, the cops would pull me over as a tactic to shake me down, hoping to find something in my car so they could arrest me for something more serious.

They knew I was on probation and could legally search me and my car whenever they wanted. So, they would pull me over, tell me to step out of the vehicle, and then take their time searching for whatever they were hoping to find.

During one particular stop, I noticed something was different. The cops asked me to step out of the car, sat me on the curb, and told me to take off my shoes. While one officer searched inside my shoes, the other officer was going through my car. He popped the air conditioner vent panel and looked down through the vents.

Because the cops immediately looked in the places where I usually kept my pistol, this confirmed for me that someone close to me must have been giving the police information. Luckily, I didn't have my gun on me that night.

Pac-Man once told me during his investigations that he and his fellow officers had given me the nickname "Teflon Jimmy." They gave me this nickname because they could never catch me dirty and never had enough evidence to charge me with some of the more serious crimes they believed I had committed.

I was able to be elusive because of the crime shows I watched on TV. When I was a kid, every Saturday at 8:00 p.m., I faithfully watched "Cops," and right after that, I watched "America's Most Wanted." I was fascinated by these criminal investigation shows and studied them to better understand law enforcement and their tactics, including how they investigated and questioned people.

I studied what the criminals typically did to avoid being arrested, how fugitives would go on the run, and what they did to evade capture. In addition, I paid close attention to where they went wrong while interacting with the police.

I learned how to deal with the cops and how the cops dealt with people who were suspects in crimes. I remember wondering why anybody would talk to the police after they were read their Miranda rights. It states, "Anything you say can and will be used against you." This was the same advice my mom gave me years ago.

During the height of my criminal activity, I was constantly looking over my shoulder for the police. I became good at spotting police cars by the lights in their front grill—two orange lights in between the two main headlights. I could hear their engines from a mile away. Anytime a car with those lights or that engine sound was coming my way, I would duck and dodge until it passed. It didn't matter if I was driving or on foot. I wanted to see the cops before they saw me. I always tried to stay one step ahead of them.

With all those traffic stops the cops were putting me through, I racked up thirteen tickets in one year. I got a ticket for almost everything you could get a ticket for.

Despite being pulled over and ticketed regularly, Pac-Man and his team still couldn't pin anything significant on me—Teflon Jimmy. I rarely paid the fines from my tickets, which would turn into warrants for my arrest. Tasha was in court with me the day they sentenced me to five months in the Orange County Central Men's Jail. I turned to face her after my sentence was handed down, and I could see the disappointment on her face. I put my head down and was led out of the courtroom in handcuffs.

I was now entering the jail system for adults. This was quite a different experience compared to the juvenile detention centers where I had spent a lot of time.

The strength of the racial politics inside the jail surprised me when I first went in. Most inmates are aligned primarily based on race or by gang affiliation. Crips are predominantly black. A white Crip, like myself, is very rare. In jail, black Crips are more likely to accept non-black Crips into their circle if they are "validated" gang members—which I was. For this reason, I surrounded myself with other Crips. The white inmates, however, do not like other white inmates associating with black inmates. Because of this racial-gang affiliation divide, I had a target on my back.

While serving my time, Tasha and I wrote letters to stay in touch. She gave me updates on Shalah.

Before my release date, I left a threatening voicemail for an old friend who was hanging out with some rivals that had recently shot a friend of mine. His mom turned that recording over to the police and the courts filed additional charges against me for terrorist threats. As a result, I was rebooked on separate charges.

Tasha was not happy to hear that I would spend more time locked up and not out helping her with our baby. She wanted me to do better. She would tell me to get my life together so we could enjoy our baby. "Jimmy, you need to do something productive with your life. We have a child to take care of." I wanted to do the right thing for us, but I didn't know how to change. I was so emotionally reactive and made my decisions based on those emotions instead of based on logic. For all the good things happening in my life, between having a baby that I loved, starting over again with Tasha, and being accepted into her family, my extended jail sentence couldn't have happened at a worse time. While I was locked up, I was hit with devastating news.

Chapter 9

LIL RON

Lil Ron was one of my best friends. When he started to hang out with me and my homies, he didn't realize what he was getting himself into. He never committed crimes with any of us or joined our gang. He was there to kick it, chase girls, smoke weed, drink, and have a good time.

Lil Ron and I met through a mutual friend while hanging out at a park. This friend was good at stealing fifths of alcohol. After she introduced us, she asked, "What do you guys want to drink?" We said something like E&J or Seagram's Gin. Before you knew it, she was back with the alcohol she stole from the grocery store.

After that first night in the park, Lil Ron and I exchanged numbers and became good friends. Having conversations with Lil Ron was different from what I was used to. He was a good person. Lil Ron was the friend I turned to whenever I needed to kick back, chill, and laugh.

Lil Ron and I talked about life and what we wanted to do with our lives when we got older. Mom loved Lil Ron, too. He was always hanging out with me at our apartment.

We liked to cruise in my '67 Buick to Hollywood. One time when we were coming back from Hollywood, Lil Ron and I got a New York City-style pizza and placed the pizza in the car's bench seat between us. We cruised around, smoking, laughing, and eating that pizza. That's what I remember most about Lil Ron—we just laughed all of the time when we were together. He was super laid back, easy to get along with, and humble. We would always joke, "Let's get a sack of weed, go back to Hollywood, and get some more of that New York pizza!"

One of my most memorable times with Lil Ron was when we took a trip to Las Vegas on New Year's Eve to ring in 1995. We took the Greyhound bus with our friend, Rabbit.

While at the Los Angeles Greyhound Station waiting to depart, we had a camera and wanted a picture of the three of us. We walked outside the bus station and down the street, where we noticed three guys on their knees shooting dice. We waited for the right time and asked one of them if they would take a picture of us. They blew us off and told us no. They were clearly in a heated dice game. I didn't like how they ignored us and continued shooting dice. I pulled my gun out of my pocket, cocked it, and told them that I wasn't asking if they would take our picture but rather I was telling them that they were going to take our picture.

I prepared to pose for the picture. When I adjusted the gun in my front pocket, it went off. I was so high that I accidentally shot a bullet straight through my jeans. Luckily, it didn't hit me or anyone else. I gave one of the guys my camera and told him to hurry. He took the picture and then gently placed the camera on the ground. The three of them then took off running. We quickly got back into the bus station as our bus was getting ready to depart.

After a long bus ride, we arrived in Las Vegas just before midnight. Lil Ron's friend picked us up at the Greyhound station and took us back to his place, where he was having a New Year's Eve party. We had a great time that night. The following day, Rabbit and I were walking through the apartments on our way to the liquor store and heard someone shout at us, "What up, blood?" from an upstairs window.

Rabbit and I responded with some disrespectful words. I pulled out my gun and fired a shot into his window. We ran back to the apartment and told Lil Ron and his friend that it was time to leave. Lil Ron's friend asked, "Why?"

I said, "We just got into it with someone and we need to go right now."

Lil Ron's friend got his keys and we quickly made our way to his car. He dropped us off at the Las Vegas Greyhound Station. and we bought our bus tickets. We were on our way back to California. It was a short, fun, and wild trip.

Because Lil Ron was always with me, my homies started questioning his motives. They asked me why Lil Ron hadn't joined the gang. I didn't tell Lil Ron to stay away because I enjoyed having him around, but I did warn him when I heard the homies talking about jumping him in.

Lil Ron believed he could keep hanging out with us and not get jumped in—a ritual of getting beat up to become a member of a gang. That was until one night when we were hanging out with my homies and out of nowhere, they jumped him in. And, just like that, Lil Ron was now from Duce Tray.

If you were hanging out with us for too long, we would eventually jump you in, or you would be told not to come around anymore.

He didn't want that life, but he went along with it for a short time. He would still come around, but I could tell this wasn't what he wanted. Suddenly, he stopped coming around. I called him occasionally, to check on him and asked, "Ron, you coming to kick it today?"

"Not today, Slim. I'm busy."

When I talked to the homies, they asked about him. Eventually, I thought they would jump him out by beating him up again and then let him be. But I should have known better. Our motto was, "It don't stop 'til the casket drops." That meant the only way out of our gang was death.

While serving another stint in jail, I called Lil Ron a couple of times. We talked about returning to Las Vegas when I got out. Lil Ron also mentioned that he was thinking about joining the military. After that, I didn't think much about the situation between Lil Ron and the homies. I figured everything would be okay until I called Mom one day.

When she answered, she started to tell me something had happened to Lil Ron and she was getting hysterical. I could barely understand what she was saying.

"What's up, Mom? What's going on? Is everything okay?" I could tell she didn't want to tell me what she was about to say. I thought it would have something to do with Barry.

"Jimmy, you didn't hear what happened?"

"No, Mom, I haven't talked to anyone lately. What's up? What happened?"

"Your fucking friends killed Lil Ron."

"Calm down, Mom. What happened to Ron? Is he okay?" I was confused and thought Mom was exaggerating. In my mind, Ron wasn't dead. I thought the homies probably caught up with him, beat him badly, and jumped him out.

"Ron is dead. Your friends killed him."

"Wait, what? Mom, how do you know it was *my* friends?"

"C'mon, Jimmy. Everybody knows. People are talking."

"So, is he dead or not?" I was still in denial.

"Yes, Jimmy, Ron is dead. They killed him Saturday night."

It was hard to catch my breath and process what I had just heard. I couldn't talk anymore and hung up the phone. I spoke to Lil Ron just a week ago and planned to visit Vegas with him.

I went to the dayroom and found a local newspaper. There it was, in black and white. The headline read, *"Tustin Marine's Son Slain at El Toro Party."*

I read the article further—"Just another dance party in an El Toro Marine Corps Air Station community center... but this one ended abruptly when Ronald Smith, 21, the son of a Marine, was stabbed to death in a parking lot outside the party." The reality of Lil Ron's murder hurt me deeply.

A mix of emotions went through me. I was in disbelief and hurt. Lil Ron was talking about joining the military. He had a good future ahead of him. Because he came from a military family and lived on the military base, he assumed he was protected there. But unfortunately, he wasn't.

I pleaded for an early release to attend Lil Ron's funeral, but they denied my request. My release day was the day after they buried Lil Ron. When I got released from jail, I went to the cemetery to visit his gravesite. His headstone still had fresh dirt around it.

Shortly after I visited Lil Ron's grave, a few homicide detectives wearing plain clothes and badges showed up at my house to question me about the murder. "I just got out of jail. I don't know what happened to Ron. I know nothing"

When the detectives left, I was sitting in my room thinking about Lil Ron's murder. I was in a dark place. I didn't know who I could trust. One week, I'm planning a trip to Las Vegas with Ron. The next week, he's dead, and word is that my homies killed him. *My homies killed my best friend.* I tried to let that sink in but my mind was all over the place.

When I met back up with the homies, I didn't ask questions. No one was talking, either. I figured when the time was right, I would hear what happened.

Word was spreading on the streets that some members of Duce Tray were involved in Lil Ron's murder. Two of them were soon arrested, charged, and later convicted. To make matters more heartbreaking, my good friend, Rabbit, was later arrested and charged for his role in Lil Ron's death. *Rabbit, who we had spent time with in Las Vegas, was allegedly involved in killing Ron.* Again, I couldn't process that. I couldn't but help to think about all the good times Lil Ron, Rabbit, and I had together. To hear he was involved in killing Lil Ron was unbelievable. I was relieved to later find out that Rabbit wasn't the one who killed him, although I thought he somehow may have been involved.

While still trying to process all this, I got a call from a friend telling me that my good friend Lil Smoke was shot in a drive-by shooting by a rival gang. Luckily, he survived. He recovered and then moved to the east coast to be with his daughter. I was losing a lot of my close friends, aka homeboys.

I was dealing with the grief of losing one of my best friends and seeing my other friends go down for it. It was becoming harder and harder to know who to trust. I couldn't get my head straight. Except, I did feel like there was one person that I could trust more than anyone and that was Tasha. More than ever, I wanted to do the right thing for her and Shalah.

Chapter 10

RAIDED

It's now 1996. I am twenty years old, fresh out of jail, and looking for a job to support Tasha and Shalah. Finding a good job without an education and a criminal record was hard—harder than robbing a drug connection across town. Tasha was working at K-Mart, where she helped me get a job. I worked there for a short time before I got a better-paying job at a light fixture company where a friend was working. I worked on an assembly line putting together landscape lighting fixtures. My friend was worried about his reputation at the workplace. "Slim, don't mess this up, and don't make me look bad."

With this new job, I felt good about myself. I was earning money by doing a respectable job and could provide for my daughter. It felt great to make an honest living. Now that I was busy working, I spent less time in the streets.

When Tasha became pregnant with our second child, Mr. Patterson started encouraging me more to pursue my education.

"Jimmy, what are your plans for the future? Have you ever thought about joining the military?" He often treated me more like a son than just Tasha's boyfriend.

"I'm going back to school to get an education." Even though I said this, I didn't believe what I was telling him. I had no plans to go back to school but I didn't want to disappoint him by saying that I had no clue what my future held.

In the summer of 1996, Tasha told me that her father was retiring and the military base was closing. I would spend some of my time going house hunting with them. They eventually found a new model home in a developing community. Once they moved in, I spent time there with Tasha and Shalah and sometimes stayed overnight.

Barry was still the asshole he always was. He even cussed out Tasha's sister and Mrs. Patterson because they honked the car horn when picking up Tasha one morning.

I assumed Barry would cut me some slack since I was working and trying to do better. One day, when I drove up to our house, I pulled the gate locks up and opened both gate doors to park my car in the gate—this is what I always did. I jumped in my car to back it into the driveway.

As I was backing the car up, I saw Barry closing the gate. I hopped out of my car and kicked the gate door to prevent it from closing all the way. The gate hit Barry in the head. He flung the gate door again and came charging at me. I stepped back, landed a punch and he went down. We ended up tussling on the ground. I got up and started kicking and hitting him. I got the better of him this time. He got up and made his way into the house. I got in my car and left.

Later, when I talked to my mom, she told me, "Barry does not feel safe with you at home."

Yah, yah, yah. I rolled my eyes.

She took a breath. "It's best if you find somewhere else to live. Jimmy, you have to go."

I moved in with Tasha and her family into their new house.

Although I had a job and was trying to do better, I discovered that I was under police surveillance. One day after work, Tasha and I went to my mom's place to check on her and Della.

I noticed a police car parked directly across the street as we were leaving. I asked Tasha to drive, thinking that if I were driving, they would pull us over. I guess it didn't matter who was driving because as soon as Tasha pulled out, the cop got behind us, turned on his sirens, and pulled us over.

I asked the officer, "Why are you guys following me around?"

"Why would we be following you around?"

The cop called for backup, searched my car, found nothing, and wrote Tasha a ticket for failure to yield. It was Tasha's first ticket.

Before this stop, I noticed cops following me around the city in an undercover Cadillac many times. I'm sure they didn't know I knew they were following me. I was watching them, watch me. One time, I saw them out of my rearview mirror following me so I decided to take them for a ride. I took them in circles. I wanted them to know I was messing with them.

It was clear now that the police had me under surveillance and were trying to build a case. Tasha and I went down to the police station to file a complaint.

Because we had shown up together, the cops took us into separate rooms and questioned us. We found out that the police were investigating an armed robbery at the K-Mart where I used to work with Tasha. The two suspects were described as one white male wearing a wig and one black male. The vehicle description matched the car that Tasha's sister owned.

The police assumed I was the white male; Courtney, Barry's brother, was the black male; and Tanya was the getaway driver. The police were convinced that I had committed the crime and wanted to know if I had an alibi for the time when the robbery took place. I had a strong feeling that I was going to be framed for this crime. Out of all the crimes I allegedly committed, this is one I actually did not commit.

"You're trying to set me up. Please don't frame me for this crime. I had nothing to do with it." I don't think he cared.

"Jimmy, we are not in the business of setting people up."

He told me that he had recently helped free a man who had been wrongfully convicted of murder and imprisoned for almost 20 years.

I continued to plead my case. "It wasn't me. I didn't do it." Because the police didn't have any solid evidence tying me to the crime, they let me go. I left the police station with Tasha but still thought the cops would frame me for the K-Mart robbery.

A few days later, while I was at work on the assembly line, I noticed the warehouse getting quiet. It seemed like something was going on outside. As I looked toward the open entrance of the warehouse, I saw officers in SWAT gear storming in with their guns drawn.

Everyone quickly put their hands up. I was thinking that someone did something very serious and someone was going to jail. I quickly realized that the SWAT team was coming for me.

"Rumsey, get on the ground! Get on the ground, lay face down!"

What in the hell was going on?! I was surprised. I got down, and the officers cuffed me.

When I looked up, I saw my friend who had gotten me the job. He looked disappointed.

They took me to the police station and put me in the interrogation room. The same detective was there again with his partners, asking the same questions.

I told him the same thing I had told him days before. "I don't know what you're talking about. It wasn't me. I didn't do it."

I thought it didn't matter if I was innocent or guilty. I was about to go down for this armed robbery—a crime I did not commit. It felt like this was their way of putting me away for all the crimes they believed I had committed.

After they questioned me, the police let me go. I headed to my mom's apartment. When I got there, Mom told me they raided her place at the same time they came to my job. I called Tasha, fearing they had raided her dad's new home. When she answered, I said, "I just got raided by the police at work and they hit my mom's place, too."

"They raided our house too."

Apparently, they hit all three locations at the same time. Tasha told me the entire story.

Tasha was upstairs with Shalah and babysitting some other children while watching TV when she heard a loud banging noise. She headed toward the front door to see what was going on. To her surprise, she heard voices behind the front door and hesitated to open it because she couldn't understand what they were saying. Then five cops wearing full body armor with SWAT gear crashed through the front door with their guns pointed at her.

One officer threw Tasha to the ground and put his knee on her back—she was eight months pregnant. Then they handcuffed her. All Tasha was thinking about was our unborn baby and she couldn't move.

Tasha was frantic. "You're smashing my stomach! I'm eight months pregnant!"

After things had calmed down, one officer picked her up and sat her on the couch. Tasha asked to have the handcuffs removed. The officer told her she was "being detained," so he couldn't take them off. This was all happening while the other officers searched the house for evidence. The children were crying as officers escorted them downstairs.

I felt so bad that this happened all because of me and that it happened at Mr. and Mrs. Patterson's new home.

When Tanya picked me up later that day at my mom's apartment and took me back to the Patterson's home, I first noticed the smashed front door of the house. Then I saw the busted trunk and glove box on my '82 Monte Carlo sitting in the driveway. They ransacked my car, too. The police collected what they considered evidence and left everything in a mess.

Because Mr. Patterson had welcomed me into his home and treated me like a son at such a critical time in my life, I felt guilty and ashamed for bringing more unwanted drama to his family. Even though I did not commit the crime they were accusing me of, I wouldn't even have been a suspect if I hadn't been living the life of a criminal.

I was nervous about talking to Mr. Patterson about what happened to his house and family. When I saw him, I apologized and tried to explain. "Mr. Patterson, I'm sorry. I honestly did not do what they were accusing me of. I think they are trying to set me up."

He just stood there listening to me. I was expecting him to say something like, *Sorry, Jimmy, but my home was just raided, and they threw my pregnant daughter to the ground with a police officer's knee in her back and a gun pointed at her. Trouble follows you everywhere you go. Enough is enough. It's time for you to go.*

Instead, Mr. Patterson looked at me and said, "You don't have to explain. If you say you didn't do it, I believe you." He followed that up with, "You are still welcome here. You don't have to leave."

I didn't know how to respond. I didn't know how to process his response, and I was not expecting to be met with such compassion and unconditional acceptance. After all the unwanted attention I brought to his home, he still accepted me and made me feel welcome in his home with his family. He gave me chance after chance, time and time again.

A few nights later, we had unexpected visitors. We were

all at home and it was around ten at night when Tasha's brother-in-law asked, "Did anyone close the garage door?" He went out to check if it was closed and spotted two police officers in the driveway. They were snooping around Tanya's car.

Tasha's brother-in-law confronted the officers. "Hey! What's going on here?"

"There is an ongoing investigation."

Tasha's brother-in-law hollered for us to come outside. Interestingly, there was no patrol car in sight. When the two officers saw us, they talked to us briefly. We could tell that they were caught by surprise. As we started questioning them, they began walking up the street to the main road where their car was parked. As they left, we noticed they had walked to the neighbor's house, and it looked like they grabbed something out of the bushes. Their behaviors were very peculiar—not parking by the house, not announcing themselves when they arrived, and grabbing something out of the bushes. We believe that they were trying to plant evidence although that never materialized—probably because they saw us watching them.

I was still guilt-ridden about what Tasha's family had to go through when the raid happened and now this. After talking to Tasha, I told her, "It's time for me to go. I don't want to bring any more drama to your family's home." I packed up my stuff and left their house.

I was on my way back to Orange County to my mom's place where she and Barry were now living in Santa Ana.

Chapter 11

AMBUSHED

Tasha's doctor was concerned about our baby's well-being after the stress Tasha endured when thrown on the floor by the police. He decided that delivering the baby early was the best course of action.

While Tasha was delivering our baby, I was in the hospital parking lot celebrating with my homies—smoking and drinking. Mr. Patterson pulled up and gave me a look of disapproval. "What are you doing? Why aren't you up there with Tasha?"

"We're celebrating!" The look on his face told me I should be with Tasha. *How was I to know that was the correct thing to be doing?!* He shook his head, parked his minivan, and went into the hospital. I followed him shortly thereafter.

When I got into Tasha's room, she was recovering from giving birth. They brought our baby back into the room. I washed my hands and held her tight. She was so tiny and beautiful. I knew now more than ever that I had to get my life together. We named her our second baby girl, Nina.

Tasha tried to convince me to come back and live with her. I still was too ashamed to go back to her house, so I asked my mom if Tasha could move in with me until we figured things out. She reluctantly agreed and Tasha and our two little ones moved in.

After moving back, Barry, who was the same old jerk, began making us feel unwelcome. There were days when

Barry locked us out of the apartment so we would have to sneak into the detached garage to have a place for the four of us to sleep at night. One morning, Barry saw us leaving the garage and told my mom. Instead of her being angry at him for locking us out of the house, she told me that we had to find another place to live. *Unbelievable!*

Over the next several months, Tasha and I bounced from place to place with our little girls, sleeping wherever we could. We often stayed at Lynn's apartment on Minnie Street in Santa Ana. I had known Lynn since junior high school. This neighborhood was known for its heavy drug dealings and gang activity. This neighborhood was so bad that it was often on the TV show *Cops*.

Lynn was dating one of my homeboys, who was locked up at the time. A lot of the homies and girls hung out at her place. If you had nowhere else to go, this was a place you could crash if you needed a place to stay. There were holes in the walls where rats would come in at night and cockroaches were everywhere. The neighbors upstairs would drop an extension cord out of their window so that we could have electricity.

I was so close to getting away from this lifestyle and now here we were, living right back in the middle of gang violence, drugs, poverty, and criminal activity. To hustle up some money to support my family, I was committing robberies, selling weed, burglarizing homes, and breaking into cars to have more cash.

Tasha was doing her best to take care of the kids. Unfortunately, I was losing hope and slipping back into my old ways.

"What are you doing out there, Jimmy?" Tasha would ask. "I don't want any more shit to happen to you. I can't take it anymore. We have kids that need us."

"I'm not doing anything. Stop freaking out."

But Tasha knew better. Things weren't right. I was getting back to where I didn't care about my life. I felt like a failure, and I couldn't care less about any consequences I would face because of my reckless behaviors.

One afternoon, I stopped by my mom's place to check on her. Right after I got there, I received a page. When I called the number, it was my sister, Della. Her voice sounded anxious.

"Jimmy, they drugged me. Please come help me."

I asked her where she was and she mentioned she was at a motel in Santa Ana known for heavy drug activity.

I grabbed my gun and flew out the door, leaving Tasha behind with our daughters. I jumped into my Monte Carlo and drove a short distance to the hotel. When I arrived, I saw a group of guys standing together in the parking lot. Some looked familiar. As I got out of my car with my gun in hand, I heard one of them say, "That's her brother!"

As I approached the group, one of them took off running. I assumed he was the guy that drugged my sister. I took off after him. I chased him down the street. I wasn't thinking straight. I was angry and didn't want to let him get away with drugging my little sister. I had one thing in my mind and that was to kill him. I started shooting at him. He turned a corner to avoid my bullets, and he then was out of sight.

This was happening in broad daylight on a busy street. I gained some sense of reality and realized that I was attracting too much attention and getting too far away from my car. It was likely that the cops would show up soon to investigate the shooting. I ran back to my car and got out of there before the police showed up.

I sped off toward my mom's place to switch cars.

When I got there, Mom was in the living room. "Mom, Della needs help. Take me to get her from the motel around the corner."

"What?" she asked. Looking at me, she knew it was serious and knew Della needed her help.

"Let's go!"

We hopped in her car this time. I figured I could return to the scene to look for Della in an unfamiliar vehicle and hopefully catch the guy who I thought had drugged her.

Mom did not know what was happening or that I had just been there shooting at someone. I didn't tell her I was already at the motel. I still had my gun on me, and Mom didn't know that, either. When we got to the motel, there were no police at the scene yet and everyone had left.

We still couldn't find Della.

We left the motel and went back to my mom's place. I started calling around, trying to find my sister. I had known some of her friends and ended up on the phone with one of them.

"Who drugged my sister?"

He replied, "Slim, you're trippin'. We wouldn't do that

to Della. She's like family to us."

He said Della smoked some weed and couldn't handle it. Then he told me she was getting better and would be fine. I believed he was telling me the truth because I knew him well and Della didn't smoke weed.

After she had sobered up, I met her at her friend's house and asked her what had happened. She said she smoked some weed and was talking out of her head when she told me that someone drugged her.

I was furious.

"Don't ever call me for help again. I almost killed someone for nothing because you smoked some weed and thought they drugged you!"

I didn't mean what I said to Della. No matter what, I would always protect her. I couldn't believe I almost killed someone over her smoking weed.

It was only a matter of time until my actions were going to catch up with me. I was going to end up dead or spend the rest of my life in prison. The sad part of that was that I didn't care about either outcome. I was ashamed of myself, and I felt hopeless. Even my children weren't enough to pull me out of my own misery. It was challenging to keep moving forward when all I encountered were setbacks.

I still had to support my kids and make money, so I called up JP, my partner in crime, and told him I knew there was a Cadillac at a nearby apartment complex that was ripe for the taking. We put a plan together to steal it. Since JP was good at stealing cars, I was the lookout man on this one.

In broad daylight, I watched JP walk through the

parking lot, use a slim-jim to get into the car, and then break the steering column to get the Cadillac started.

Once JP drove out of the parking lot, I followed behind in his car so we could meet up with some other friends to strip the car. We took the rims, the seats, the sunroof, and the stereo system. Then we put dummy tires on the car and were on our way to dump the Cadillac in a supermarket parking lot in enemy territory.

We drove in three separate cars—JP was in the stolen car that we were dumping, I was in another car with Lil Smoke, and our friend was in a third car. It was about nine o'clock at night. We thought it was going to be a smooth operation.

To get to the supermarket, we were going in the back way—down a street, through a cul-de-sac, and then down a little path connecting the cul-de-sac to the supermarket parking lot. As we approached the drop-off spot, we noticed about ten gangsters hanging out in front of a house near the cul-de-sac. They stared us down as we drove by. This was their neighborhood and by looking at us, they knew we weren't from there.

After we dropped the stolen car at the supermarket parking lot, we were down to two cars. We headed back down the same street which we had just come from. We should have taken a different route, knowing that there were a bunch of gangsters hanging out in the direction we were headed. I was in the passenger seat of one car, and JP and our other friend were in the other car. We noticed that JP didn't have his lights on. We were worried that might get him pulled over by the police for that. To let JP know about his lights, we flashed him with our high beams just before we got to where the gangsters were hanging out in front of the house.

Just after we flashed our lights, they ambushed us. A barrage of bullets from multiple shooters hit both cars. It was like being in the middle of a war zone with bullets smacking the side of both of our cars. JP hit the gas and quickly made it through to safety.

Instead of going forward into the shooters like JP, we thought we could get out of there by going backward. My friend stopped the car and tried to throw it in reverse. As his foot slammed on the gas pedal, the engine revved to the max, but we weren't moving—the car was stuck in neutral. We were sitting ducks as bullets continued hitting our car.

There wasn't anywhere to run or hide. I quickly crouched under the passenger seat dashboard to avoid being shot through the front or side window. My friend laid down across the front bench seat for cover. Bullets were flying through the front windshield. I knew we were going to die at any moment. I was waiting for someone to walk up to the car and shoot us at point-blank range. Then, suddenly, the gunfire stopped.

They must have emptied their clips or thought they killed us and took off. This was our chance to escape. My friend popped his head up to get a glimpse of the street ahead of us and threw the car back into drive. He punched the gas pedal to the floor. I stayed under the dashboard as we sped through the street as fast as we could.

Miraculously, we made it out. Later that night, my friend

noticed a hole in his jacket hoodie and a bullet hole in the driver's seat headrest. He was inches away from being killed.

I was getting shot at more and more frequently, and I believed it was only a matter of time before I got hit.

Chapter 12

KARMA ON KILLER CORNER

Tasha, the girls, and I moved into our first apartment in Tustin. We had just received assistance from a program that helped homeless people, and it covered the down payment for the apartment. It wasn't long before word got out about where I was living. I saw rival gang members frequently driving through our apartment complex. It seemed like I was the only one catching the backlash from what my homies and I were doing.

One day, Rabbit, Courtney, and I were outside my apartment complex fixing the car stereo in my Monte Carlo. We noticed some rivals, who we recently had an altercation with, driving by my apartment. There were three of them in the car, slowly driving by and mad dogging us.

The person in the passenger seat leaned over, looking as if he was reaching under his seat for a weapon.

At that moment, the apartment security guard was walking in our direction and stopped to make small talk with us. The security guard was unaware of the intensity that was building at that moment between us and our rivals.

When our rivals saw the security guard stop to talk to us, they kept driving, staring us down as they drove off. Although they didn't know which apartment I lived in, I worried that my family was in danger.

On October 3rd, 1997, Rabbit came to my place to check on me. As it got late, I walked Rabbit outside to say our goodbyes. Tasha and the kids were inside. We were standing in front of my bedroom window near the parking lot when we saw some rivals from a different gang pulling into the complex. They lived in the same complex as me and my family.

We knew who they were. They shouted some disrespectful words from the car. Rabbit and I shouted back at them. This time I had my gun on me.

As the disrespect escalated, I said to Rabbit, "Let's not do this here. My kids are inside."

As Rabbit was about to take off, he asked if I was okay for him to leave.

"I'm good, Rabbit. Come back tomorrow and we'll take care of it."

"Yeah, I'll be back tomorrow," Rabbit confirmed.

The next day Courtney, Rabbit, and a friend of Rabbit's showed up at my place. We started smoking, drinking, listening to music, and planning our move against the rivals from down the street. Once it got dark, the four of us walked across the street into the alley where our rivals usually hung out.

I stopped to talk to an older friend who was in the alley. He was usually there drinking with others but wasn't a part of a gang. I asked him where everyone was—he knew I was looking for the rival gang members. He could tell that we were up to no good. He attempted to talk some sense into me, saying, "Slim, you got kids. It's not worth it. Let it go." As much as I respected him, I wasn't hearing him. I was still mad about the disrespect that Rabbit and I had received the night before.

We couldn't find anyone from the rival gang, so we walked a few more blocks to a place known at the time by the police as "Killer Corner." It was given that name because there had been a murder on each street corner at that intersection within one year. This was also in the heart of our territory.

The Circle K was on that corner and we went in there to get some more alcohol. As we were leaving the store, two cars sped into the Circle K parking lot and stopped right in front of us. It took me a moment to see the people inside.

Once my eyes focused, I noticed they were rivals from Santa Ana. When the passenger closest to me exited the car, I saw a nickel-plated revolver in his hand. I'll never forget the look in his eyes as he pointed the gun at my face from about ten feet away. He had a cold evil look on his face. I could see his pain.

I froze while looking down the barrel of his gun.

Then without moving the gun away from my face, he pulled the trigger.

Remembering now what happened then is near impossible—it is all a blur. From what I have been told, I fell back and smacked my head on the concrete. I was laid out on the sidewalk in front of the store, going in and out of consciousness, choking on my blood, and fighting for air. People were screaming all around me. I could not move, could barely keep my eyes open, and could barely breathe.

As I laid there with blood pooling in my mouth, I felt like I was drowning. I was fighting for my life and trying to keep my eyes open when Courtney returned to help me. I was gasping for air.

He crouched over my head, screaming at me.

"Keep your eyes open, Slim! Don't close your eyes! Slim, open your eyes! Keep fighting!"

Courtney was holding my head and turning it to the side to clear my airway from all the blood that was filling my mouth. Blood was pouring out all over the ground. I started to breathe a little easier once I wasn't choking on my own blood. Courtney stayed by my side. I grabbed onto his arms as hard as I could as I fought to stay alive.

Soon, the police rushed into the parking lot, and someone said an ambulance was on the way. Then a police officer yelled at Courtney.

"Put him down! Put his head down! Put him down and back away, now!"

Courtney screamed back at the cops.

"He can't breathe! There's blood in his mouth! He needs help!"

Courtney made the bold decision to disobey the cops. He stayed there and held onto me. I was lying on my back and trying to keep my eyes open.

Racing through my head were images of my two daughters. Chances were slim that I would survive, but I know that it was the thoughts of my daughters that gave me the strength to keep fighting for my life. I was telling myself to fight for them.

While in our apartment, Tasha had heard the sirens but didn't think anything of it. She was with our two kids and her sister, Shanise, when Rabbit called her and told her what had happened.

"Jimmy's been shot. It's bad. He's in front of the Circle K. Call Jimmy's Mom."

Tasha's heart started to race.

Immediately, Tasha called my mom and relayed the information.

"Jimmy just got shot. He's at the Circle K."

Tasha called MoMo for a ride, and MoMo sped over to the apartment. On her way to get Tasha, she passed the Circle K and saw the police cars and the ambulance. She picked up Tasha and headed back to the Circle K.

With Courtney's help, I was holding on until the paramedics arrived. They quickly assessed the gunshot wound, strapped me to a gurney, rolled me inside the ambulance, and rushed me to the hospital. As Tasha and MoMo pulled into the Circle K parking lot, the ambulance sped away with me in it. They chased the ambulance to the hospital.

I arrived at the hospital in critical condition. The medics rushed me to the emergency room where the doctors and nurses immediately got to work.

Everything faded to black.

Word about what happened to me was spreading in the streets. Those who were at the scene and knew me told everyone they knew. *Slim is in the hospital. They shot him in the face. He is in serious condition and might not survive.*

Out of pure coincidence, another young man was shot in the head earlier that night in a separate gang-related incident. He didn't make it, and the news of his death was unsettling to everyone at the hospital. People were concerned that I would suffer the same fate. Friends and family prepared for the worst.

Chapter 13

IN GOD'S HANDS

After worrying about my condition for hours, doctors came out of the operating room with good news.

"He is going to pull through."

Tasha and Mom were relieved to hear that I would survive and walk out of there. The doctors then informed them that I was lucky and my road to recovery would be long.

Tasha remained at the hospital for the rest of the night. At one point, she walked over to the hospital's chapel, sat in a pew, prayed for my life, and then wrote a letter to God.

The following day, while I was still unconscious, *The Los Angeles Times* ran this story: "TUSTIN—A man was shot in the face after a possible gang fight in a convenience-store parking lot early Saturday night. Jimmy Rumsey, 21, of Santa Ana was rushed to Western Medical Center in Santa Ana where he was listed in critical condition Sunday."

The doctors had put a halo brace around my head to hyperextend my neck. This was screwed into my skull. While I couldn't turn my head, I could see from my periphery that someone was sitting next to me. I was in and out of consciousness from all the pain meds, and I thought that maybe I had died. As I focused, I saw that a nun was praying over me.

I thought I was about to meet my maker. Why else would a woman of God be praying over my body? Little did I know that Tasha had put in a prayer request for me when she had visited the hospital chapel.

As I lay in the hospital bed on a respirator, the doctors tried to figure out how and where to operate. My chin slowed down the impact of the bullet that lodged in the C-4 area of my spine. The bullet tore through my face and throat. My throat swelled and clogged my airways. They also discovered that the lodged bullet caused the carotid artery in my neck to be ninety-five percent closed.

I'd wake up in pain and fade back into sleep. When I came to, I tried to figure out what had happened to me but would quickly lose consciousness again. I was told that family and friends visited me during that first week. The police also came to question me but realized there was no way they could get any answers from me while I was in that condition. Pac-man was one of those police officers that came on a few occasions.

After about a week, my condition stabilized, and they transferred me to another hospital for more surgeries and rehabilitation. The doctors first performed mandible surgery to fix my chin. They inserted a titanium plate to put my chin back together and wired my mouth shut after surgery for it to heal. I then underwent an angiography procedure where they cut near my groin and injected ink into my bloodstream to make sure my blood was circulating well.

Up until this point, the bullet remained in my spine. The doctors conducted more tests to determine if the bullet was moving. The bullet was near my nerves and a major artery. They knew that if they tried to take it out, the bullet might slip into the wrong place and could paralyze or kill me. They decided it was too dangerous for them to remove the bullet and believed that I would have a better chance of survival if they could stabilize it inside of me. The bullet remains lodged in my neck to this day.

Detectives from the Tustin Police Department reappeared at the hospital, aggressively fishing for information about what had happened at the Circle K. The detective asked who shot me. They wanted me to tell them what I knew and said that they wanted to find the guy who did this to me.

I was in no condition to talk or provide them with any information—not that I would if I could. They asked Tasha if our kids needed anything, offering diapers and food. I made it clear to Tasha that she should not take any gifts from the police and should not tell them anything.

As I got stronger, the police returned to question me again. The detectives were relentless, hoping that I would eventually crack under pressure and give up the identity of the guy who shot me. Again, I knew that talking to the cops about any crime was an unwritten rule of the gang lifestyle. I told them I remembered nothing and refused to cooperate with them.

In the back of my mind, I wanted the shooter free, so I could find him when I got out of the hospital and get revenge.

After about three weeks in the hospital, I tried to check myself out voluntarily. I was still in severe pain and barely had the strength to walk or even take off the hospital gown.

I cautiously slipped the gown off, put my clothes on, walked up to the nurse's station with Tasha, and told the nurse that I was ready to check out. She informed me that my insurance wouldn't cover my medical bills if I checked myself out of the hospital against medical advice, and, at this point, my hospital bill was going to be very expensive—hundreds of thousands of dollars.

Easy decision made—I went back to my room and put on my gown.

While I was stuck in that hospital bed, I had so much time to think. The night of the shooting would not stop racing through my mind. I couldn't help but wonder about all of the different scenarios that could have unfolded.

What if I had stayed in the store a few minutes longer? What if I had gone back into the store when I saw them? What if I had run as soon as I saw them pull up? Would they have shot at me? Would they have hit me? If I had been shot anywhere else, would I have survived? Why did God keep me alive?

I also thought about what I would do to the guy who shot me. Would I let him get away with it? Should I retaliate? Would I be putting my family in more danger by fighting back? Would staying quiet make me seem scared? Would I get caught and be taken away from my family to spend the rest of my life in prison?

When I thought about the possibility of losing my freedom, my daughters' faces flashed through my mind. Now that I had two daughters, who would be there for them if I wasn't around? What would happen to them? Would they end up with a stepdad who abused them like Barry did to me? I couldn't stand the thought of them going through that. And, what about Tasha? She had always been there for me, always accepting me, and always caring for me. How could I leave her? How could I risk making her a single parent? Hadn't I put her through enough?

Something dawned on me during one of those nights in the hospital. I saw flashes of the shooter's face the moment right before he pulled the trigger. I could see his pain from the look in his eyes that night. I decided to pray for him. *Wasn't there something in the Bible that said love your enemies, do good to those who hate you, bless those who curse you, and pray for those who mistreat you?* I asked God to protect him. My heart vacillated between wanting to kill him and wanting to pray for him. Praying for my enemy was something I had never done but it started to feel more and more like the right thing to do. I knew I was changing but I wasn't sure who I would become. There was one question that I kept asking myself—*What would I do with my second chance at life?*

After nearly a month in the hospital, they finally released me. They unscrewed the halo that hyper-extended my neck and sent me on my way. I had a long road of recovery ahead of me.

Chapter 14

THE PATTERSONS

Tasha and I knew that we could not continue to live in the apartment we were living in when I was shot. My rivals knew where we lived and, in my physical condition, there was no way I could protect my family. So, she and Mr. Patterson packed our stuff and moved it to his house. As much as I wanted to move in with her and start over with the Patterson's support, I was worried that trouble would follow me there again. Tasha and I decided it would be best for the family for me to recover at my mom's place.

Once I was settled at my mom's, some of my homies showed up and asked if I was ready to ride again. I was in no condition to be in the streets looking for payback. I was in a weak state. My mouth was wired shut, and I was in a lot of pain. Even though I was six feet tall, I only weighed 120 pounds. I was not about to leave the house looking for revenge.

While at my mom's place, I slept on the couch. Barry left me alone for the most part but he didn't stop fighting with Della. One night, Barry was yelling at her so badly and acting as if he might hit her. Although I was in no condition to be fighting, I went to the kitchen and grabbed the biggest knife I could find. Barry ran out of the house as fast as he could. Once again, Mom told me I had to leave.

Tasha had said she was done with my gang-banging lifestyle. She had been asking me to move back to her family's house and get away from the chaos at my mom's place. She said that Mr. Patterson was in support of me living with them again. I decided to do what Tasha had asked me to do, and I moved in with the Pattersons.

Shortly after I left my mom's place, her and Barry's fighting had finally reached a boiling point, and they broke up. I was so glad to hear Barry left and that he and my mom were finally done with each other. I felt a huge sense of relief knowing that my mom and Della were safer without him there.

While living with Tasha and her family, I learned a lot from watching how Mr. Patterson interacted with his kids. I learned a lot about what it takes to be a father. I watched how he talked to his daughters. He spoke to them with love and listened to them with understanding. I saw him give them attention. I saw how his daughters respected him and not because they feared him but because of how he treated them. There was a mutual fondness among them all.

Living with Tasha's family this time was what I desperately needed.

I started seeing Tasha in a new light. She was always there for me and never hesitated to tell me how much she loved me. I wanted more and more to spend the rest of my life with her.

I planned a surprise for Tasha on the day before her 20th birthday. I took her to get her nails done and then we drove to the beach. We walked along the boardwalk holding hands and talking about our daughters and what our future could look like. When we got to a bench, we stopped to sit down for a while.

We sat there and talked some more about life. It was so peaceful hearing the waves crash against the shore and smelling the ocean breeze. It felt so calm to be there and to be with her. Finally, I slowly got down on one knee. Her eyes widened with surprise. I expressed my love to Tasha. I explained how much she meant to me and that I wanted to spend the rest of my life with her. She started shaking and crying. Then, with a ring in my hand, I asked her if she would marry me.

She said, "Yes!"

When we got home, Tasha's parents were having a party. She looked for her parents in the crowd of people. As soon as she spotted them and knew she had their attention, she shouted to everyone, "He asked me to marry him!"

Everyone cheered.

Jokingly, Mr. Patterson asked, "Why didn't you ask me to marry my daughter?"

A little later, I pulled him to the side and asked him if I could take him and Mrs. Patterson out to eat sometime so we could talk.

He laughed it off and said, "Yeah, Jimmy, we can do that. Thanks for asking."

Within the next few days, I took Tasha's parents to Denny's and gave them a speech about how much I loved Tasha. I told them I would always do my best for her, love her, and protect her. I told them that I didn't even think of asking Mr. Patterson for his permission to marry his daughter before asking her. I explained that I really didn't have any role models or guidance on how to propose, and I apologized if what I did seemed disrespectful. As forgiving as always, Mr. and Mrs. Patterson said that they understood and were not at all upset with me.

Then, with much sincerity, I asked if I had their blessing to marry their daughter. Luckily for me, they said yes. I thanked them both.

"Jimmy, you're family. You can call me Pops now," Mr. Patterson assured me.

After I proposed to Tasha in 1998, things started looking up. Mrs. Patterson helped us by co-signing for an apartment in our new community. Finally, we were living on our own as a family. It felt good to be a dad, raising our kids on our own. I was so happy to be engaged to Tasha—the woman who always had my back and loved me unconditionally. There was a sense of peace and happiness when I was with my family.

Tasha enrolled in school and worked part-time at a department store while I stayed home with the kids. I was proud of Tasha for going to school and working so hard to provide for us. Once again, she showed so much strength. But, at the same time, I was humiliated because I could not provide for my family and had to rely on my fiancé to do it. I eventually went to a temp agency and took odd jobs that didn't pay much. After work, I would come home in severe pain and migraine headaches because of the bullet lodged in my neck.

I was having trouble sleeping. I was restless and had dark thoughts at night. Luckily, I happened to get a job working the graveyard shift at an inventory company. I would work during the night taking inventory at different stores. This was a good fit for me as it helped me avoid the darker thoughts. I would come home from work and be able to fall right to sleep. I was starting to understand how my bad choices as a youth affected my life as an adult.

Still, I missed my friends. I occasionally went back to the old neighborhood to see them. Tasha was not happy about me going back to my old territory. Whenever I returned, she and I argued.

"Jimmy, something bad will happen to you if you keep going back out there. Every time you're with them, something bad happens."

I didn't listen to her, and I kept going back.

Chapter 15

CHANGING AIN'T EASY

I was once again slipping back into my old ways, often meeting up with some of my homeboys. Lil Smoke had moved back to California and lived close to my new place. One afternoon, he and an old friend came to pick me up. We decided to eat and have some drinks at a Mexican restaurant in Moreno Valley. We also decided to ditch without paying the bill.

Afterward, I told my friend to take us to Orange County. When he realized how drunk I was, he said, "I can't take you, Slim. OC's too far. This is my dad's car and he needs it back soon."

I was drunk and not in the mood to hear someone say no to me.

I told Lil Smoke to give me the gun.

Lil Smoke passed the gun to me in the backseat.

With the gun in my hand, I told the driver, "I'm not asking you to take me. I'm telling you."

He turned his head around. "Slim, no! I need to take the car back to my dad."

Then he turned the radio up and headed in the opposite direction of where I told him to take us.

I cocked the pistol and fired one shot into his stereo from the back seat. The gun blast shook us all up in the car. Now that I had the driver's complete attention, I said again, "I'm not asking you to take us. I'm telling you!"

He turned the car around and headed towards Orange

County. We exited the freeway in Tustin and immediately noticed a police car behind us.

As we took the next left, heading towards Rabbit's house, the cops hit us with their blue and red lights.

As the driver came to a stop in the middle of the street, I gave the gun to Lil Smoke in the passenger's seat.

"Put this in the glove box."

I looked out of the windows and saw two cops approaching both sides of the car. One of them was Pac-man. That's when I heard one officer say, "Rumsey's in the back!"

This was the first time the cops had seen me since I had been shot. The cops knew this wouldn't be a routine traffic stop with me and Lil Smoke in the car.

They asked the driver for his license and registration. The driver told Lil Smoke to get the registration out of the glove box.

Not good!

Lil Smoke slowly opened the glove box, trying to keep the gun hidden. One of the officer yelled, "GUN!" They drew their pistols on us immediately.

I looked out the window to my right and Pac-man's partner had his gun pointed straight at my face. I told him to get his fucking gun out of my face.

"Shut the fuck up!" he screamed back. "Put your hands where I can see them! Put your hands in the air."

They ordered us out of the car one at a time. The driver went first, then Lil Smoke, and then I was the last one out of the vehicle.

Lil Smoke, the driver, and I were all searched, handcuffed, and arrested. Then the questioning began. Lil Smoke and I knew the drill and didn't say a word. We were all taken to the police station and learned that the driver told the entire story of what happened that day, including the food run we did at the restaurant in Moreno Valley. He told the police that the gun was mine, that I kidnapped him, and then made him drive us to Orange County.

I was almost charged with kidnapping, but the DA decided not to pursue those charges. They believed the kidnapping charges wouldn't stick in court since the driver was affiliated with our gang.

While at the police station, they started questioning me again about who shot me at Killer Corner. The police were still investigating and trying to build a case against the suspect. They already had an idea of who it was. They told me I was either going to jail for being a gang member in possession of a loaded firearm, which is a felony, or I could cooperate and walk out of there a free man.

They then showed me a picture of the man they believed shot me. I looked at the picture. Then, they asked me if he was the guy who shot me.

"No, that's not the guy who shot me."

The police told me that the word on the streets was that he was the shooter. But, because it was hearsay, they needed an eyewitness. I refused to answer any more questions, and I was on my way back to the county jail.

While they booked me into jail, the police officers handed me over to the county deputies and told them to keep me away from the Watergate Crips.

One deputy asked, "And why should we do that?"

The officers responded, "Because they just shot him and he still has the bullet in his head. He's from Duce Tray Crips."

The deputies chuckled and one of them said, "Okay. We'll put him upstairs with the skinheads. They'll knock the bullet out of his head." They all thought that was pretty funny. I thought that they were idiots.

I had accumulated a lot of enemies during my lifetime. Because of this, I knew I had to be prepared for anything in jail. Truth be told, I still was in no condition to be in any physical altercation. My chin was still healing from the metal plate that had been put in there.

They placed me in an eight-man cell. There were four bunk beds, a table, and one toilet.

Once I got situated in jail, I called my mom to tell her where I was. It took me a day to work up the nerve to call Tasha and break the news to her. I was disappointed in myself for putting myself back in this situation. It had only been a few months between getting shot to almost dying to being arrested on a felony charge and to being locked up again. Maybe the deputies weren't the idiots here.

My grandma's words on her deathbed came to my mind, "Jimmy, please stay out of trouble."

I let her down. I let Tasha down. I let Mr. and Mrs. Patterson down. I let my daughters down. I let myself down.

I couldn't help but think about my mom and all the time

she would cry because I broke her heart.

I turned to God and began talking to him more and more. I began praying for the strength and the power to change my ways for the better. After all my prayers, I could feel something inside me changing. I felt tired—tired of hurting my family, tired of hurting people, tired of being hurt, tired of being locked up, and tired of not giving a fuck.

Being with Tasha and my kids was the life I wanted. They meant the world to me. But, if I didn't change my ways, I might lose the opportunity to live the life I dreamed of with my family. It was within my grasp, but it was about to slip right through my fingers. I had been given a second chance and I blew it. I wasn't sure if I could get another one.

I told myself that I would never return to jail once I got out and that this lifestyle was over for me. I knew I had said this before. I hoped that I meant it this time.

Mom gave her all to deal with the new felony charge and hired an attorney. A guy from New Jersey had long hair and a cowboy hat. He walked and carried himself like his shit didn't stink and he was a know-it-all, good ol' boy. He tried to persuade me to take a plea deal, which included jail time, a felony charge, and probation. It didn't sound like a good deal to me, but he pushed for it anyway.

My attorney put me on the spot in court when I wasn't ready to take the deal. The judge called my name and read over the deal agreement. He asked me if I understood the charges and agreed with the terms of the plea deal. I replied in front of the courtroom, "No, I don't agree to the deal."

My attorney looked at me, surprised. He thought I

would take the deal if he put me on the spot. But the judge gave us some time to talk privately.

"Jimmy, I know why you don't want to take the deal. You don't want to take the deal because you don't trust yourself. You know you'll violate your probation and end up back in jail."

My attorney and I discussed a new plea deal that he took back to the District Attorney. The deal was that I would plead guilty and then I would receive a sentence that included time served and three years of formal probation with gang terms. This meant that I couldn't associate with gang members, visit gang territories, wear anything gang-related, or participate in any gang activities. Additionally, if I violated the terms of my probation, I would go straight to jail. I was assigned regular check-ins with my probation officer for the next three years and had to submit to drug tests, go to anger management classes, and be subjected to random home searches.

When the attorney told me that the DA accepted the deal, he smirked. I don't think he believed I could make it through the probation terms with no violations. I looked him straight in the eye and told him that I was never going back to jail.

I had Tasha in my corner, two kids who needed me, and the support of Tasha's family. I had to reprogram my way of thinking and start making better choices to break this cycle. The old me had to be buried and I had to embrace the change. It wasn't easy, but I started making better decisions. I would do whatever it took to be with my family. I had to put them first.

Chapter 16

THE STRUGGLE IS REAL

I struggled with post-traumatic stress disorder, depression, and paranoia. There were many sleepless nights. I had recurring nightmares of people trying to kill me. In my mind, I kept replaying in my mind the night I got shot and nearly died.

I struggled with not being able to provide for my family financially. We depended on government assistance. I felt hopeless when I thought about starting a career because I had a criminal record, no high school diploma, and now a disability. We were struggling every month to make ends meet.

We were on the waiting list for Section 8 housing—a federal program to help low-income families. A year later, we got approved. Unfortunately, the apartments we lived in at the time of approval didn't accept Section 8 as payment, so we had to move.

We were in a race against the clock to find a new place to live. We had 60 days to find a place that would accept Section 8. Unfortunately, not many places would accept Section 8 because of its stigma—people on the Section 8 housing program were thought to be lazy and disrespectful of the property they were renting. Several of the landlords we talked to turned us down because of it. Finally, we found a place and settled for a run-down apartment complex.

Tasha started working at a daycare center after she obtained her early childhood certificate. She was working to become a teacher. Tasha would sometimes take our kids to work with her when I was in too much pain to care for them.

Tasha and I were approaching our one-year engagement anniversary. We asked Pops and Mrs. Patterson to take us to Las Vegas, where Tasha and I tied the knot on January 11th, 1999. We celebrated getting married over the weekend and returned home as husband and wife. Life was better. I was still on probation but managed to stay clear of the police and out of jail.

Life was not so great for Lil Smoke, one of the few homeboys I would still hang out with. He was shot for the second time in a drug deal that went bad. Like me, he was lucky to survive the shooting. He and I would meet up from time to time but would now keep a very low profile. We would stay at my house and play Madden football on an old PlayStation.

One day we were hanging out and drinking with Lil Smoke's neighbor who suggested we drive to the mall. We hopped in the car and headed out. I sat in the back seat. Lil Smoke and his neighbor were in the front and started arguing about something. They were not paying attention to the road. The traffic light was red as we approached the intersection. Before I could say anything, we headed straight through the intersection into oncoming traffic. I grabbed onto the seat in front of me to brace myself. Then bam!

We crashed into a car in the middle of the intersection and our car spun out of control. I looked up and saw the other car end up on the curb, in front of somebody's yard.

After the spin-out, our car was still in the middle of the street.

With my adrenaline pumping, I didn't know how badly injured I was. The next thing that crossed my mind was I had violated my probation by hanging out with Lil Smoke. We both weren't supposed to be associating with any gang members. If we got caught, we would both go back to jail.

With that in mind, I opened the door and took off running. I looked back and saw Lil Smoke and his neighbor exiting the car. Lil Smoke hobbled away on his crutches in the other direction, back towards his house.

I hid in a nearby restaurant and used a payphone to call Tasha. I told her about the accident and told her to quickly come to get me. She was not at all thrilled with me.

"Of course, you are in trouble again. I am on my way."

When Tasha arrived at the restaurant to pick me up, I asked her to swing back around toward the accident, so we could check out the scene. As we were pulling up, there were cops and paramedics everywhere. I saw how bad the accident was. The paramedics were attending to the woman who was driving the other car. She appeared to be okay.

After the collision, my back hurt but I thought it would go away so I didn't see a doctor about it. The back pain became worse instead of better as the days went by. A few weeks later, I felt a shooting pain going down my back and leg. Still, I just dealt with the pain and hoped it would eventually heal on its own. Unfortunately, my condition only got worse.

My mobility was limited, which made it difficult to get

around the apartment. We wanted a bigger place to live with better living conditions. Occasionally, the gated community across the street from our apartment complex would leave the gate open. We would drive through the gate and look at the houses, wishing we could afford to live there.

One day, we saw a house for rent and hoped that we could rent it. It was a small one-story, three-bedroom home. It was perfect for us because we were expecting our third child.

We completed a rental application with the owner but knew there was a slim chance we would qualify for the house. The owner of the house was hesitant because of our need to use Section 8 housing assistance. He asked us a lot of questions.

Then he said, "If everything you are telling me is true, then I'll rent it to you."

He gave us a chance.

This was big news for us. We were happy and things were finally going our way. We moved in shortly after and Tasha gave birth in October 2001 to our third daughter, Janee. Shalah and Nina were starting school.

I was nearing the end of my probation. I didn't have any problems with the law for three whole years. This was the longest I had stayed out of trouble since I was eleven years old.

We had a little extra money, and our first wedding anniversary was coming up. We had never been able to afford any sort of couple vacation. So, I looked up places for us to go to locally. I found a resort in San Diego and reserved a room for two nights.

The resort was beautiful. It had a fishpond and parrots surrounding the garden area that would talk to the guests. Our room was right on the water overlooking a bay. We spent time on the *Bahia Belle,* a party boat that cruised around the bay with live music. We ate at a good brunch buffet with jumbo shrimp and food we had never heard of. At this resort, we tried almost everything. It was great!

We even bought matching tennis outfits, rackets, and shoes so that we could play tennis. Of course, we never ended up playing tennis, but we had a great time and felt good about ourselves.

This was our first taste of the good life, and we knew we wanted more.

Chapter 17

HOPE

We were finally feeling a sense of normalcy when Tasha's cousin and his friend decided to visit us from Chicago. Like most people, when they came to California, they want to see the sights in Los Angeles.

We took off one Saturday night toward Hollywood. We pulled off the freeway onto the Sunset Strip. We drove a few blocks and stopped at a red light. Hollywood was jumping with a lot of people, and we were ready to have a good time.

While we were at a red light waiting for the light to turn green, we felt and heard a loud crash. The back window of our car shattered from the impact. Our car rolled forward and hit the car in front of us. We got rear-ended by a truck traveling at a high speed. The driver was so drunk that he didn't even attempt to step on his brakes.

We all got out of the car and looked around. I saw the drunk driver trying to start his truck back up. He was attempting to flee, but his truck wouldn't start. I walked over to him, reached through his window, and took the keys out of the ignition. He tried to leave on foot after I took his keys, but Tasha's cousins, along with some other people, grabbed the driver, put him back in the seat of his truck, and kept him there until the cops came.

The ambulances arrived shortly after that, and they took us all to a nearby hospital, where we stayed overnight. My pre-existing back issue and the bullet in my neck only worsened my injuries.

After being released from the hospital, I had to see additional doctors for the pain. I could barely stand up straight, and I had to use a cane or a wheelchair to get around. I couldn't sleep at night because the pain was excruciating, and it hurt every time I moved. I needed epidural injections to manage the pain.

After years of battling for Social Security Disability Insurance (SSDI) benefits, I finally saw an administrative law judge in court. The day of the hearing was stressful. I desperately needed medical insurance and financial support since I was now disabled and couldn't work. We left the hearing uncertain about my chances of being awarded SSDI.

It was six weeks before we heard anything. Then, when the court's decision arrived in the mail, Tasha and I opened the letter together. To our surprise, the judge ruled in my favor. They approved me for SSDI with back pay.

Even with my disability benefits, we were still living paycheck to paycheck. We couldn't afford to eat out much. Tasha and I sometimes argued over what we could afford when we ate out. When we wanted cheese on our burgers, that cheese could be why we over-drafted our account. We were that broke. Tasha would say, "We have cheese at home."

Through a turn of events, we were lucky to catch a break. We happen to respond to an advertisement for German rottweiler puppies.

We showed up at the address, and the house looked like a mansion. I noticed some nice older model Cadillacs in the driveway. It was the lead drummer's house from a very successful band. A lady at the house was selling the puppies. I had the pick of the litter and picked the biggest male I saw.

While maybe not the best financial decision, we purchased the rottweiler for $300 and named him Raider, after my favorite football team. Raider was black and mahogany with a big block head, and according to his paperwork, he was from a German champion bloodline.

We hadn't planned on breeding him, but after all the compliments, I thought we would give it a try. We bought a female rottweiler and named her Coco. Because of their pedigrees, I knew their puppies would be valuable. For a while, we bred rottweilers to make some extra income.

While walking Raider and Coco around the neighborhood on my mobility scooter, I met a guy named Mario. We talked for a while and I found out he was from Santa Ana. We immediately made a connection.

Mario had bought a home across the street from the house we were renting. He was still living in Santa Ana and had purchased the house as an investment property. I asked him what his plans were with the house. He said he was going to rent it out.

It was a two-story house much bigger than the one we were renting. We were also looking for a bigger place to live because Tasha was pregnant with our fourth child.

Mario asked me if we were renting or buying the house that we lived in. I laughed. We were so poor we could barely afford our current place on Section 8 housing assistance.

I said, "We rent."

"How much do you pay?" Mario asked.

I told him how much our rent was and explained that we were on Section 8 and were lucky to be living here.

"I'll rent you my house for the same price you're paying now." He even said Raider and Coco could live there. I was shocked.

When I got home, I told Tasha the great news. She didn't believe someone would rent a bigger house to us for the same price we were paying and accepted Section 8. She thought that there had to be a catch but there just wasn't. So we accepted Mario's offer and moved in.

I remained in contact with Courtney after he moved back to Kansas City. He moved after I was shot. I often thought about him and how he returned to the scene of the shooting to help me that night when I almost lost my life. I decided to take a flight and go see him. He said he wanted to move back to California, and I told him he could stay with us until he found a place.

I returned home from my trip and Courtney was soon on a bus heading back to California to take me up on my offer.

Courtney was a people-person, and it didn't take long for him to become friends with our neighbors. One of my neighbors owned a business and offered Courtney a job. It felt good to have Courtney around again.

Chapter 18

THE CALM BEFORE THE STORM

It was now late in 2005, and we occasionally visited my mom's sister and her husband in Los Angeles during holidays. This was the only family I had left after my grandma passed away. They lived near where my father and mother grew up. While visiting my aunt and uncle, my dad's name came up. I asked my uncle if he knew how I could find him.

"The only way you're going to find him is through his mother—your grandmother."

My uncle told me he knew where she lived.

"You better hurry. She's getting old."

It was worth a try.

My uncle confirmed that the address we looked up in the phone book years ago was the correct one. We held onto that address but never knew how to approach the situation.

My biggest dream had always been to meet my father. In my mind, we'd meet and be happy to be reunited. He'd tell his wild tales of when he was sailing the Atlantic Ocean, and I'd tell him my crazy stories. We'd laugh, we'd bond, and we'd become father and son again.

Over the years, Tasha and I would watch talk shows about families being reunited. We reached out to some of those shows but with no luck. I even wrote letters to the addresses we looked up on the internet linked to his name, but I never heard from anyone.

It was always a huge letdown. I had all but given up on

finding my dad until I talked with my uncle that day. If we were ever going to find him, the time was now.

Given that my mom always said he was dead or in prison, I believed it. However, I wasn't sure I was prepared to know the truth. With those thoughts etched into my mind and this being my biggest dream, I couldn't bring myself to go, so Della and Tasha went to the house without me to find him.

When they arrived at the address, Della walked up to the house and knocked on the door. No one answered. As she walked back to the car, a neighbor saw Della and came out to greet her. He was curious about who she was and why she was there. He asked her, "Can I help you?"

Della said she was looking for our father, whose mother lived at the address. The neighbor said he had been living next door to her for twenty years and didn't know she had a son. Della gave our phone numbers to him, and he agreed to relay the message to the woman who lived there.

It crushed my biggest dream when my sister and Tasha returned and told me that the woman at the address did not have a son. I remember thinking that my mom was right— he was dead or in prison.

The next day, Courtney and I walked to a local restaurant to have breakfast. As we were walking home, my cell phone rang. The number didn't look familiar. I answered it. The person on the other end asked, "Is this Jimmy?"

"Yeah, who's this?" There was a long pause.

"This is your dad."

I stood there on that street corner with Courtney in complete shock and disbelief.

My Dad was alive and free!

I thought I would never see or hear from him again, but here I was, on the phone with him after 25 years. It was surreal. My emotions were all over the place.

He asked many questions, and I could tell he was trying to feel me out. He asked me where I lived and what my life had been like. I told him I'd been in a lot of trouble with the law growing up, but I was doing much better.

He laughed and said, "I thought you would've grown up as a little Catholic boy because of your grandma." Then he asked, "What did your mom tell you about me?"

"She told me you had got yourself into some trouble and were on the run from the law and that you were probably dead or in prison."

After listening to me and understanding that I wasn't the "church boy" he thought I would be, he felt more comfortable with me and explained his situation.

"You're my son and I'll be honest with you. I feel I can trust you and that you won't turn on me. What your mom told you is true. I did get myself in trouble with the law and I'm trying to clear it up now."

After talking to him for a short while, I told him I wanted to meet him. I asked him where he was living.

"I'm close by, living near San Diego. You're not far from me. You and Della should come out to visit."

I agreed.

When Mom found out that Della and I were going to

141

meet our father, she had a bad feeling about it. She was worried that he might have a trick up his sleeve. If anyone knew Dad well, it was my mom. She decided that she would come with us.

The three of us showed up at the restaurant where he told us to meet him. A man was standing in the parking lot in front of a pickup truck. His hair was combed back. He was wearing jeans, a blue polo shirt, and brown work boots.

Mom said, "There he is. That's your dad."

I could see his resemblance to me. He looked sun-tanned and his facial features seemed worn—he looked as if he had a hard life. I was in disbelief that I was meeting him.

We parked the car and got out. Mom hugged him and then he hugged Della. My dad turned to me. We embraced each other for a long time. Everyone was shedding tears of joy, but I could tell Dad was a little on edge. He was constantly looking around. He seemed paranoid as if someone was going to show up and arrest him—I knew the feeling; I knew the look.

We headed inside the restaurant and sat down at the table. The look on Dad's face showed that he was shocked that we were all together. It had been twenty-five years since Mom took me and Della and left Dad and Sheree behind. We had so much that we wanted to catch up on.

"Dad, I want to show you a picture of my family." I was eager to see his reaction to my interracial family. If he wasn't accepting of it, then I didn't plan on trying to build a relationship with him.

He looked at the pictures and said, "You have a beautiful

family."

"Dad, I never forgot about you and Sheree. If it wasn't for Tasha, I may have never found you. She's been helping me look for you for the past seven years."

"What an amazing woman you have," Dad said. "I would like to meet her one day."

I asked Dad about my half-sister, Sheree. I had some old pictures of the two of us from when we were younger. Sheree was always on my mind as I was growing up.

I wanted to know where my sister was and how she was doing. Dad said she was doing well and living in the state of Washington.

"Can you connect us?" I asked.

He agreed and gave me her phone number.

I was excited to call her and looked forward to reuniting with her.

I shared with Dad the things I had gone through while growing up. Of course, he was not expecting to hear the stories I told him, like how I grew up in and out of juvenile hall, that I was a gang member, and that I had been shot in the face. He took it all in but didn't have much of a reaction.

I could tell he was holding back because Mom was there. He kept shifting in his seat. His face was like stone. It seemed as though he did not want to reveal too much to us. He looked uncomfortable. Throughout the meeting, he seemed serious and rarely laughed. When we finished eating and talking for a few hours, we said our goodbyes and took some pictures to capture the moment of our family reunion. Dad told us he would be in touch and wanted to see us again soon.

He called me later that night, drunk and slurring his words. He expressed how happy he was that we finally reunited. His personality was definitely different from earlier that day.

After our conversation, I called Sheree. I wanted to reunite with her just as much as I wanted to reunite with Dad. I really missed her.

When I called, she answered the phone. I couldn't believe I was talking to my sister after all these years. I never thought I would talk to her again. We talked for hours, catching up on life. It was almost as if we had never lost time.

Sheree told me she was married and living with her husband and son in Washington. Sheree had a good memory. She remembered us playing on the docks. She said she remembered the day we left her and Dad—a day she said she'd never forget. The pain of us leaving was seared into her memory.

By the end of the call, we both expressed that we were eager to see each other again. Sheree soon flew to California for us to be reunited. Sheree, Della, and I met at a restaurant and had a fantastic time. It was a special moment for us, full of reminiscing, catching up, and laughter. Since this time, we have remained in close contact and have met each other's spouses and children.

Dad and I continued to talk every day. He would call me to tell me stories about his life and ask for stories about mine. He told me that he too had spent time in juvenile hall as a kid. At first, it seemed that our mutual trouble with the law was something that bonded us. Later, it started to seem that he put too much emphasis on it—as if it were something to be proud of.

Dad called me one night and asked if he could meet Tasha. He was clear that I was not to bring mom again.

He told me to meet him in San Diego at the boat docks. It surprised me that Dad was still hiding on a boat. Tasha was pregnant with our fourth child when she came with me to meet Dad. We walked through the harbor, found his sailboat, and boarded it. The three of us talked about our lives while Dad and I drank some beers and had a few shots of Jack Daniels. During our time together, Dad showed a lot of love to Tasha. He kept saying how extremely thankful he was for her helping me find him.

Dad showed me his ID with a fake name and birthdate. No wonder it was so hard for me to find him before.

As we talked, Dad chugged beer after beer. I could tell that he liked to drink. Before leaving his boat that day, Dad asked if me, Tasha, and the kids wanted to spend a night with him on the boat sometime.

"Sure! That sounds fun."

This is what I had been dreaming about—building a relationship with my dad.

When we brought the kids to meet my dad, he told us to meet him at an address different from where we had met him before. This time, Dad picked us up in a dinghy boat on the shore and took us out to the water where his sailboat was anchored.

Dad took us for a cruise around the bay. It was a beautiful day with perfect weather and calm water. Dad let Tasha, the kids, and I steer the boat. He had a grill on the boat and made us a steak and lobster dinner. It was turning out to be a great day. He noticed it was hard for me to move around on the boat because of my back pain and offered us his bed. Dad kept cracking beers open, sometimes drinking the cans in what seemed like one gulp. He became pretty drunk. I tried to ignore it.

As the sun set and it was becoming darker, Dad anchored his sailboat and invited me to cruise around the harbor in his dinghy. He said Tasha could just stay on the sailboat with the kids.

While I thought it was a bit odd to take another cruise around the harbor at night, I got in the dinghy, and we puttered out toward the Pacific Ocean. The big U.S. Navy ships docked in the harbor were towering on both sides of us. I could barely see a thing, but Dad seemed to know where he was going.

Dad was quiet and very drunk. He was my father, but I hardly knew him. Once we got close to the ocean, he stopped the boat, turned towards me, and squared his chest.

"Give me the guy's name who shot you," he said. "I got connections. Let me take care of this for you."

So, this was what the dinghy excursion was all about.

It caught me by surprise that he would try to strong-arm me for the name of the man who shot me. He hadn't mentioned any of this before.

"Don't worry about it. It's already taken care of."

Dad pressed the question again. "Is this guy still alive?"

"Yeah, he's still alive."

"I want his name."

"I don't know his name."

"I know you know who he is. Give me the name, Jimmy."

He was getting more aggressive. *What in the world was happening here? We were just supposed to be having good family time and this turn of events felt very odd.* If I had been my old self, I would have reacted differently to Dad's attempts at bullying me, but I responded non-aggressively.

"Look, Dad. The last I heard was that he's in jail."

"I find that hard to believe. How do you not know his name but know he's in jail?"

He was now challenging what I was saying instead of picking up on the social cue that I was uncomfortable with this conversation and didn't want to discuss it. I felt things might get physical by how he responded to me.

I had to figure out what to say so that I could get back to the sailboat with Tasha and the kids. To shut him up, I gave him the nickname of the guy who shot me and said that's all I knew about him. He fired up the dinghy and took me back to the sailboat. We rode back in silence in the dark, with the sound of the engine pushing us through the water.

When we returned, Tasha saw the look on my face. She was concerned.

"Is everything okay?" she whispered.

"We'll talk about it later."

I wanted to grab Tasha and the kids and leave. But we

were in the middle of the harbor with Dad as our only way back to shore. There was no way of knowing how he would react if I asked him to take us back to land before it was time to head home. Clearly, he was unstable. Because the kids were with us, I wanted to keep things as non-confrontational as possible so we could get home without them getting scared. After what happened out in the dinghy, I knew I needed to watch myself around him. Mom was right. He was still shady.

We cautiously interacted with Dad as he kept drinking throughout the night. I noticed that the more he drank, the angrier he became. Tasha, the kids, and I were stranded on his boat. I had been too quick to introduce Tasha and the kids to him. I had been too trusting because I wanted so much for him to be a good dad.

As the night dragged on, it was clear he was still furious at my mom for taking his kids from him. He blamed her for the things I went through as a kid, like my time in juvenile hall, the abuse I took from Barry, and how I almost lost my life from gang-banging. Of course, he didn't take any responsibility for how his criminal behavior caused my mom to leave him. Maybe if he would have been a better person then my mom would have stayed with him. Maybe my mom, Della, and I wouldn't have gone on to live a life with Barry's abusiveness.

"How does your mom feel about this?" Dad asked. "How does she feel about all the shit she put you through?"

"She did her best. I did this to myself."

"No, Jimmy. It is her fault. She should have done a better

job raising you. If you had stayed with me, you wouldn't have gone through all that."

"I don't know, Dad. Maybe I would have."

By this point, he was slurring his words and unable to focus his sight on anything. He had a blank look in his eyes. After more complaining about my mom, he finally passed out. I thought about trying to sneak Tasha and the kids into the dinghy to get us back on land, but I didn't know how to start the dinghy, and I thought things might take a turn for the worse if my plan failed. I was in a lot of pain and physically limited so wasn't quite sure that I could overpower him if I needed to do that.

I got little sleep that night as I tried to figure out how to get my family safely back to land before he woke up. I just hoped that he would be different after he slept off the drunkeness.

Dad woke up early and made coffee for us. He then took us back to shore as if nothing had happened the night before. He had been so drunk that I wondered if he even remembered. After spending the night with Dad, I felt uncomfortable around him, especially out on the water.

He would still call me just about every day after that. When he would call me sober, he always expressed his love for me, and I knew it was sincere. He would call me and leave songs on my voicemail about father and son relationships. He said he used to listen to those songs and think of me.

But when he called me and was drunk, he would angrily talk to me about whatever was on his mind. Most often, it was about the bad things I had gone through and how he wasn't happy about my upbringing.

Despite his behavior, I tried to accept him for who he was and build a relationship with him. I knew that I wasn't perfect and needed a second chance, so I tried to be understanding of his shortcomings. The times we had when he wasn't drunk were so good, yet so different from the times that he was drunk.

I allowed Dad to come over to our house. When I was able to be on land and have more control over the situation including the amount of beer we had in the house, our times together were good. There were many times when he would stay the night with us. We were trying to build a father-son relationship, and it seemed to be working as long as he didn't drink excessively.

One time, I thought it would be a good idea to bring my dad to my mom's place for dinner. I hoped that perhaps they could forgive each other for what happened between them. While the dinner seemed to go smoothly, later I realized that reuniting them was a huge mistake.

After that dinner, my dad called my mom and belittled her. Little did he know, I grew up hearing men talk to my mom like this my whole life. Dad was more similar to Barry than he knew. I was not about to let another man, especially my dad, talk to my mom like this.

During one of our phone conversations, he started bad-mouthing Mom again. I pushed back.

"Dad, get over it. I don't appreciate you disrespecting her like this."

"What a pussy! I always knew you'd grow up to be a momma's boy." He was drunk again. I didn't let him off the hook this time, and we exchanged heated words.

Please, God, not another asshole!

My biggest dream was turning into my worst nightmare.

Chapter 19

BIGGEST DREAM, WORST
NIGHTMARE

After I confronted my dad about my mom, he started calling me and leaving threatening voicemails on my answering machine. The things he said were very hurtful.

All the trauma that I had been through with father figures in my life came to my mind. Because Dad was my biological father, it hurt me even more. I always thought that once I found my dad that he would be the one to help me.

Not long after his threats, Tasha and I were at the Patterson's for dinner. Dad kept calling me repeatedly while Pops and I were playing dominoes.

I kept ignoring his calls and the voicemails kept piling up. During a pause in the domino game, I checked those voicemails to see what was so urgent and why my dad kept calling me.

The voicemails were nothing but threats against my family and me.

"I'll have some bikers show up at your doorstep and they'll bring you to me. I'll take you to the middle of the ocean and introduce you to God, boy." *Why do assholes call me "boy?"*

It was heartbreaking to hear my dad threatening my life. I was reaching my breaking point.

Dad's calls kept on coming. I could tell he was wasted.

In his last voicemails, he taunted me, saying, "Hey boy, where are you? I'm over here at your sister's house. Where's your little cub scout homeboys now?"

Della didn't know Dad was calling and threatening me. I was getting worried that he might hurt her or her family. I interrupted the game of dominoes and told Pops that I had to take care of something.

I told Tasha that we needed to go.

Dad was bringing out the worst in me, and my mind went blank. *Who did he think he was, threatening my family and me?*

I drove with Tasha to our house and grabbed my pistol grip shotgun. We then headed straight to my sister's house. On the way there, Tasha repeatedly asked me, "Are you okay? Is everything alright? What's going on? Why do you have your gun?"

I didn't say much in return. My mind went blank. I was infuriated and focused on getting over there to confront Dad.

When we pulled up to Della's, I saw Dad's truck parked in front of her house. I walked up to the front door with the shotgun by my side and knocked.

Della answered. When she opened the front door, I looked past her and saw Dad lying on the carpet on the living room floor. When I saw him, I barged through the door, through Della, and walked straight toward him.

I didn't want to give him a chance to get up, so I put the shotgun barrel directly in his face, pinning him on the carpet. He laid there, stunned with a drunken stare. "Say what you were saying now! Say it to my face! Talk that shit now. Don't be a bitch. Say it!"

I was doing the same thing he did to me over the phone, but now I had a shotgun in his face. I was in such a rage from what he had done to me and stood there confused about what was happening. *How did we get to this point? This is my dad.*

The scene was chaotic. Everyone was scrambling to get in between us. All I could hear in the background was Tasha, Della and her family screaming frantically.

"Jimmy, no! Don't do it! Don't do it, Jimmy!"

My dad remained silent, staring at me as I stood over him. I would have pulled the trigger if he had said something back to me. I almost killed my dad at my sister's house in front of my family that night.

Instead of pulling the trigger, I said, "If you ever threaten my family or me again, I'll come find you and nothing will stop me from sinking your piece of shit boat with you in it, you piece of shit drunken sailor. Fuck you! Try me!"

Then I pulled the gun up, turned around, and left the house with Tasha.

Not even ten minutes passed after we got home when, what do you know, Dad was calling me again. I answered this time.

"That was a nice little toy you have there, boy," he said. "Too bad you don't have the balls to use it!"

This dude is crazy. I was still furious.

I jumped in my car and returned to Della's house with

155

Tasha. I left the shotgun at home this time, fearing I would kill him. I was hoping to get him outside so I could kick his ass.

I knocked on my sister's door with no shirt on to show everyone I didn't have a weapon. "I don't have a gun," I told Della. "Tell him to come out here."

He refused to come out.

"Jimmy, please just leave," Della said.

Because it was Della, I did as she asked. He was lucky she was trying to protect him.

I didn't know what to expect from my dad after that. I thought that maybe one day he would come after me and try to retaliate.

After that incident, I was sure that Dad and I could never build a relationship. I couldn't trust him anymore and he probably felt the same way about me.

I regretted ever meeting Dad. I wished meeting him would have remained a dream. After that day at Della's, he stopped calling me, which was for the better.

I had a different dream to focus on. Our son, Lil Jimmy, was born on September 21st, 2005.

As I became a father to a son, I thought deeply about my strained relationship with my father. I told myself I would never do anything to hurt my son and make him feel the way I felt about my father.

I swore I would be a good father to my son.

About a month later, while Courtney and I were hanging out in Orange County, I checked my phone and saw I had several missed calls from Tasha. I listened to her voicemail.

"Jimmy, hurry and get home! Your dad is here! Janee let him in the house when I was upstairs. He saw her in the window and gestured to be quiet like he was surprising us. I came downstairs with Lil Jimmy in my arms, and he was already in the house, standing in our living room. He wants to talk to you in person. You need to get back here now!"

Not this again.

I hurried home, and sure enough, Dad was in my house with my wife and kids. I didn't know why he was there, and I didn't know if he had a gun on him. He seemed to be in a calm state of mind when I walked in.

Dad looked at me. "Son, can we go for a walk and talk?"

I hesitated to answer.

"I'm sorry for what I did," he said. "I would like to talk to you alone."

I figured the best thing to do was to get him out of my house and away from my family so I agreed to take a walk with him.

As I left the house with him, I whispered to Tasha to lock the doors and not unlock them until I returned without him.

On our walk, Dad stopped me.

"I'm sorry, Jimmy," he said. "What I did was stupid and wrong. I shouldn't have done it. I love you, son."

"Yeah, I'm sorry, too. I just can't have this shit in my life," I said. And I meant it. I wanted a good life with solid relationships.

After that, we slowly gave our relationship another shot.

Over the next several months, Dad and I talked over the phone, and I even invited him over to my home again a few times to have dinner and hang out with us.

Dad continued to express to me on multiple occasions how grateful he was to have found me, how much he loved me, and how he wanted me in his life. He stopped drinking around me and our relationship improved.

He opened up to me and told me how he grew up and was physically abused by his father. His father used to beat him severely. Hearing these things helped me understand him better.

But once he became comfortable around us again, Dad started drinking again. I also discovered that Dad wouldn't accept Della as his daughter. He wanted nothing to do with her, and that bothered me. He said my mom had cheated and that Della may not be his.

I figured it was best to get him out of our lives. I slowly distanced myself from him and do not have a relationship with him to this day.

I suspect a lot of people who had absent fathers later find out that there was a reason that they were absent—mostly because they weren't good dads. Before I had met him, I had envisioned him being my superhero and rescuer from the abusive life I lived with Barry. In the end, I found out the truth. While it broke my heart, I had to put that fantasy to rest.

Chapter 20

REDEMPTION

Getting to know my father was very eye-opening. He was the complete opposite of Mr. Patterson. My dad was an abusive alcoholic. Mr. Patterson was a man of dignity and showed unconditional love to his children. I now strive to be much more like Mr. Patterson and be the father that I wish I had. I always tell my kids how much I love them.

I continued to be a stay-at-home dad and focused on raising my children to the best of my ability and with lots of love. After ten long years, Tasha received her bachelor's degree and teaching credential.

We experienced several significant events that pointed toward things getting better. We moved into a nice suburban community with great schools. It felt like an enormous weight had been lifted off our shoulders. It was such a blessing. We were getting a taste of the American dream.

Tasha landed a teaching job as an Education Specialist working with students with mild to moderate disabilities.

Our kids continued to excel academically, and we were very involved in their education. Every time they came home with good grades or an award, we made a big deal about it.

I reflected on the life I had growing up and saw how the environment in which I lived contributed to my delinquent behaviors. I had very little adult supervision and felt as if no one really cared about me except my homeboys. I knew that I didn't want that for my kids. Instead, I tried to provide a home environment where they felt loved and accepted. I showed them that I would be there for them through their successes and failures. Tasha and I tried to provide stability at home so that they could thrive in the outside world.

As Lil Jimmy grew up, we signed him up for sports like baseball, football, and basketball. I helped coach all the teams he played on. It was a good feeling to have a good relationship with my son, teach him, support him, love him, and watch him do great things with his life.

My favorite times with my family were family movie nights, which I learned how to do from Pops when I first met Tasha's family. I would yell, "Family movie night!" And the kids would get excited and bring blankets and pillows to the living room. Nothing felt better than sitting on the couch with them, laughing and bonding together—most of the time, I didn't even pay attention to the movies we were watching. Instead, I would sit back, look at my family, and be in awe. *What did I do to deserve all of this?*

Everything that I had been praying for over the years was happening, whether it be for financial stability, for my kids to be in decent neighborhoods and schools, or to be a healthy family with a strong bond. Of course, it didn't occur overnight, and it didn't happen when I wanted it to, but eventually, it all started to come together.

There was a time when Tasha was laid off from work. While we struggled a lot financially, we were able to roll with the punches because we were in it together. Compared to the other challenges we had faced, we knew that we would figure it out as we went along and come out on the other side of this better than we were going into it. Unfortunately, we were forced to file for bankruptcy. We also got the news that we were expecting another daughter. Courtney was born on May 12th, 2011.

We knew we needed to figure things out fast. Tasha started a tutoring business, and an idea that I had for several years started to become a reality.

For years, I wanted to get my life together and help kids from my community. I wasn't sure though if the community that I had taken so much from and had done so much damage to would even allow me back in.

Could Jimmy Rumsey positively impact other people's lives? It was something I wondered about and was sure that the community would too. I knew my heart was in the right place.

In March 2015, I received a text message from Frostee. He attached a *Behind the Badge* newspaper article.

The article was titled, "A Look Back at Tustin Police's Original Gang Unit:Those Were the Hot Years." It described the "peak crime years" during the 1990s in Tustin. The article featured Pac-Man, the officer who gave me the name "Teflon Jimmy" and another cop who always tried to put me behind bars.

The article was a sign. I saw it as an opportunity to make my way back home to help the youth.

I decided to track down Pac-Man's email address. He was now a lieutenant in the Tustin Police Department. After a couple of days of wondering whether I should reach out to him, I figured that I didn't have anything to lose in doing so. I didn't even know if he'd reply to me after all these years. It was nearly twenty years since I had any run-ins with the Tustin police.

I sent the email to Pac-Man with the subject line *Killer Corner Survivor!* I explained to him I was not the same person I once was. I told him that Tasha and I were married, that I was a father of five, and that my kids were thriving in school.

I expressed my desire to give back to the community. I told Pac-Man that I wanted right my wrongs by helping young people avoid taking a similar life path that I had taken.

I waited for a reply. In my mind, it was a slim chance Pac-Man would respond to me—Jimmy "Slim" Rumsey.

To my surprise, Pac-Man returned my email. He was shocked to hear my life had completely turned around for the better and that I was dedicated to helping the youth. He asked if I would be interested in a follow-up story to the original article in Behind the Badge about the gang unit they had just published. I was hesitant at first. I clearly had never interacted with the police in a cooperative manner and this would be new for me.

I talked it over with Tasha.

"Jimmy, don't you think this is a chance to clear your name and do what you've been saying you want to do?"

With that, I decided to meet Pac-Man.

I was nervous as I entered the building. Whoever would

have thought that I would voluntarily walk into a police department motivated to do good? I saw Pac-Man. I stuck my hand out to shake his, and he pulled me in for a hug.

"Jimmy, I never thought I'd live to see the day."

"Yeah, man, me, neither." I laughed.

When the follow-up article was published, it received a lot of attention. The response was overwhelmingly positive.

Over the next few months, Pac-Man arranged for me to do a few community presentations, so I could express my goals of helping at-risk youth. He also set up multiple speaking engagements for me. I spoke at Hillview High School, the continuation school I once attended.

I shared my story everywhere I got the opportunity. It was a surreal moment in my life. I had a lot of work to do and had to back up what I was saying.

I spoke in front of people from the Tustin Chamber of Commerce and the Kiwanis Club, to name a few. I even gave presentations with my formal rival, Justin, who shared the same goals and passion.

I could tell that Pac-Man was supportive of my return. He told me he would do whatever he could to help me, but that I would have to be the one "putting in the work." After Pac-Man trusted I was sincere and saw that my actions backed up my words, he was enthusiastic about guiding me in the right direction. He welcomed me back to my hometown and opened many doors for me to fulfill my dream.

It didn't take long for people in the community to hear I was making my way back. Of course, some people doubted me because of my past. I couldn't blame them, but I wanted to prove through my actions that I was sincere.

Word circulated and more people heard what I was doing. News of my efforts caught the attention of one person in particular—someone who I never expected to hear from.

Chapter 21

FORGIVENESS

I was on the football field helping at Lil Jimmy's playoff game when I began receiving text messages from JP, my once partner in crime.

"Is your heart in a good place?"

I wrote back, "Yeah, I'm good. What's up?"

I waited for him to relay bad news.

"Someone is standing here with me and he wants to talk to you."

"Sure. Whoever it is, have him call me."

The phone rang.

"Hello. What's up? What's going on?"

JP let this person call me from his phone.

"I read the article about you. You have a beautiful family. You're a good man, and I'm sorry for what I did to you. I'm sorry for the trauma I caused you and your family."

His voice was shaky, and I felt his pain. It was a similar pain to what I saw that day when he held his gun to my face and pulled the trigger.

He apologized over and over again.

"I'm asking for forgiveness. That's why I'm calling you."

"You're already forgiven. I have no ill feelings toward you. I've been praying for you, and I hope you're doing well."

We talked for a few minutes and then I told him I was on the football field at my son's playoff game. I asked him if I could get back to him after the game.

"Yeah, of course."

After I got off the phone with him, my son caught a pass and ran the ball forty-five yards for a touchdown. The coaches were high-fiving. Everyone was jumping around and screaming with excitement. Some of them looked at me as I stood there, unable to celebrate, holding my phone in my hand, and staring out onto the field.

I scanned the stands for Tasha and signaled to her that I was going to call her phone. I dialed her number.

"The person who shot me just called and asked for forgiveness."

After a moment of silence, Tasha replied, "What?" She couldn't believe it.

"I know. I'm as surprised as you are."

We tried to make sense of everything as we drove home after the game. "How do you feel about this, Jimmy?"

I told her that receiving that call gave me the closure that I needed. After I got home and processed everything, I called him back to finish our conversation.

Before we hung up, I asked him if Tasha and I could meet in person. I wanted to let him know face to face that I truly forgave him, shake his hand, and embrace him with love.

We agreed to meet at a restaurant in Santa Ana the following week. When I let Tasha know about our meeting, she was nervous about my safety. She was worried that the meeting might not go well or that it might be a set-up.

"Jimmy, are you bringing your gun?"

"God's got us covered. We don't need it."

Tasha looked at me like I was crazy.

"Well, then I'll bring the Glock."

She put the gun in her purse. I smiled. Just like Tasha, she had my back.

I reached out to JP and asked him to come to the meeting. On the day of the meeting, my wife and I were the first to arrive at the restaurant. JP arrived shortly thereafter. A guy wearing a big coat walked through the front door towards us. I recognized him right away. I stood up at our table as he walked toward us. He walked right up to me and we both embraced each other.

"I have been dealing with this for so many years. I'm sorry for what I did."

He was sickened by what he had done. The shooting weighed heavily on him every day since he pulled the trigger.

"We all did shit in the streets that we wouldn't have done if our life circumstances had been different," I said. "If it weren't you, it would've been someone else. It's over now. We're done with all that. We're good."

After that, we ordered some beers and food and talked about how we'd been living over the years. Like myself, he had a hard life and faced many challenges growing up. We stayed at the restaurant talking for a couple of hours. When it was time to leave, we all got up, walked outside, and he and I embraced each other again. We committed to staying in touch. Before we parted ways, I said, "Let's make something good out of this situation."

He nodded, "Yeah, let's do that, Jimmy."

After we left the restaurant, Tasha told me that she was surprised and relieved that the two of us got along so well. She smiled and said that she was glad that she didn't have to use the Glock.

After I processed that meeting, I asked my family if they were open to meeting him and forgiving him. Of course, they were open to it.

I asked my mom how she felt about extending her forgiveness to him. I told her that even though he made a terrible decision that night, I believed he was a good person and had a good heart.

"Jimmy, if you forgive him, then so do I. I would be happy to meet him and tell him myself." Mom also conveyed to me that she was glad I was finally finding peace in my life after all these years.

I called my new friend to ask if he was open to meeting my family.

"I would love to do that." He asked if I would meet his mom as well.

I responded in the same way. "Yeah, I would like that." We decided to meet at the same restaurant where we had met before. When my mom finally met him, she gave him a big hug. They talked and shed some tears of relief and happiness. I stood there looking at them and taking it all in.

We then set up a meeting for me to meet his mom. A few days before Christmas, Tasha and I were invited to his mom's house. She was such a sweet lady. While we had the tea and cookies that she made for us, we shared details of our lives.

It's strange to think that my life was saved on the night when I almost lost it. I guess a shot to the face and a slim chance of survival can really make one evaluate their life. It is sad to think that I had to come so close to death to realize that I had a lot to live for. At the same time, I am grateful that God had a bigger plan for me that night, and his plan made me a better father, a better son, a better husband, a better friend—a better person.

EPILOGUE

My life is very different now compared to how I grew up in this world. I didn't think I would make it to my twenty-first birthday, and I know that it is surprising to many that I didn't end up dead or in prison.

But, now, with Tasha as my wife and best friend, we have a wonderful family. Being a father has been and will always be the best part of my life. I am so very proud of all of my children.

My oldest daughter Shalah, usually the life of the party, graduated from high school with honors. Her spirit is free, and she lives to the fullest. Growing up, she said she wanted to be a flight attendant, and now she spends time flying from city to city experiencing so much of what this world has to offer.

My second daughter, Nina, also graduated with honors. She was awarded a scholarship to attend nursing school at Hawaii Pacific University (HPU). On the night we went out to celebrate, I made an excuse to my family about needing to make a phone call before I went into the restaurant. After my family went in ahead of me, I sat in the car and cried with overwhelming emotions. I cried tears of pure joy.

My third daughter, Janee, always brought home good grades and received many academic awards growing up. She is humble, hardworking, and loves sports. I see a lot of myself in her. Janee played four years of high school basketball and helped her team to win the California Interscholastic Federation (CIF) championship game during her senior year. Since graduating, she has been working hard and was recently promoted to a manager position at her job.

My son, Jimmy Jr, is a great young man. He has a great personality and a great outlook on life. He is always looking out for others. He plays football for his high school and works when he's not busy with school and football. He also received an academic college scholarship and plans to use that next year to follow his dreams of becoming a software engineer.

My youngest daughter, Courtney, was obviously named after the man who saved my life. She is my little lovebug. She watches football with me and tags along to classic car shows with me. She has learned to cook from her mom and is amazing at it. Courtney is independent, smart, and loved by everyone she meets. There's no doubt in my mind that she will do great things with her life.

We provided an environment for our children where they felt secure in their relationships with us. Not that we are perfect by any means, but we try our best to be loving, supportive, and predictable. Whether they succeed or fail, our children know we are there for them and accept them. We hope that this has given them the confidence they need to become successful individuals. They can go out and explore the world without having to worry about what is happening back home.

As part of my own healing, I was introduced to an organization called Project Kinship. The mission of this organization is to provide support and training to those impacted by incarceration, gangs, and/or violence. This is done through the provision of hope, healing, and transformation.

I started attending Project Kinship's weekly healing circle on Tuesday nights. It was here that I discovered that I could heal from my traumas. I learned that I didn't just have to live with the pain caused by my trauma, but I could work through that pain. By being vulnerable and talking openly about my traumas, I started to heal.

During my time at these meetings, I shared that I wanted to work with at-risk youth—those that had lived a life similar to what I had lived. I believed that I could make a difference based on my experiences. An opportunity presented itself to me where I could actually start to make a difference and give back to my community.

Through Project Kinship, I became a Restorative Practice Intervention Specialist in the Santa Ana Unified School District and started to work in the schools with at-promise youth.

We advocate for students who need support and provide various other services, including gang intervention, conflict mediation, one-on-one mentoring, campus safety, community intervention, and conferences with students and families.

We also take students on field trips and hikes. We visit the beach, attend professional sporting events, and tour colleges. Outside the schools, I work with and support youth to help them during their time in juvenile hall and their transition back into the community.

One of my proudest moments doing this work was being a part of one of the first anti-human trafficking projects in the California Public School System, where students, teachers, and staff took a stand against human trafficking on our campus and in the community.

I've received recognition for mentoring youth at Sunburst Youth Academy. Sunburst Youth Academy is Southern California's premier residential leadership academy for teens. This free program helps youth develop the self-confidence, discipline, life skills, and education necessary to become successful adults and fulfill the potential they have within themselves.

In 2019, Project Kinships honored me with the Heartbeat of the Year Award for my dedication and care for the youth.

In 2022, I was recognized by Operation Warm Wishes as an individual making a tremendous difference in the community.

I am motivated in my work to be the person in these youths' lives that I needed when I was growing up.

Through this work, I see positive, life-changing outcomes. Many students earn their high school diplomas, attend college or trade schools, join the military, and use the tools provided to them to lead successful and productive lives.

I recently received a letter from one of my students. He was an active gang member and in survival mode every day. He had no interest in his education, missed 77 full days of school, and failed all his classes. Not to mention, his home life was chaotic and dysfunctional.

During his freshman year of high school, I started working with him. I encouraged him and told him not to give up hope. I told him that he had to put in the work to reach his full potential.

It wasn't an overnight change for him. It never is. But eventually, he finally had gotten in enough trouble that he started to turn his life around to work toward a positive future.

I noticed his grades improving, which gave him confidence. He started attending school every day. Then one day, he received an award from the school district for Outstanding Student Attendance.

I told him this was a huge accomplishment and asked if he was excited to be invited to the ceremony to receive his award.

"No, Jimmy. I'm not going to go. I'm starting to feel like a nerd."

Knowing he had little support, I offered to go with him. It took some time, but eventually, he agreed to go to the ceremony.

When we got there, I could tell he was uncomfortable. We sat and listened to the names being called, and when they called his name to go up to the stage to receive his award, he put his hoodie over his head, as if he was embarrassed that he was being recognized for doing something good.

He returned, handed me the award certificate, and said, "You can keep it, Jimmy." While embarrassed, I could tell he was proud of himself and didn't need the piece of paper to know that he was doing well.

This was just the beginning for him. While walking around campus, he told me he added a seventh period to his schedule to catch up on credits. These extra credits would be enough to allow him to graduate from high school.

Our conversations turned to his plans for his future, which included going to college, pursuing a career, and chasing his dreams. I couldn't believe what he was telling me. It was such a beautiful thing to witness his transformation right before my eyes. I was so proud to see him grow from the person he once was to the person he was now becoming.

He wrote me a letter before he graduated high school.

Dear Mr. Rumsey,

It's been a minute, My G, and even now it feels crazy that we are even here. You remember when you used to say that it will get better, but that I needed to change? Back in sophomore year when everything was popping off and the school decided to bring in counselors to help impact the youth in better ways, I was one of many that were put in the program, and it necessarily helped me see the truth. To this day I don't really know what made me change but I do know that some part of it had to do with what you told me. The person I've become is not the best person, but it matches my style. I used to be a gangbanger in my days, but now I've reformed to be an eighteen-year-old adult going to college and working. My plans are to get my first bachelor's degree, but starting at the community college level and working my way up. My education won't stop until I feel like I'm done.

I am writing to you today because my senior English teacher has asked us all to reflect on our last twelve years and find someone who has made an impact on our lives and write to them. Yo Jimmy, I just wanted to thank you for all the things you did even if I didn't listen at first. If only I would've realized it sooner, I could have stopped myself from digging the hole deeper. At least I know now that you can only trust a certain few and not to let anybody stop you from living your life. At school, you would tell me to just get it over with so then you could be done but I didn't. Not until I hit rock bottom. Once I fell to the bottom, I finally understood what I needed to do. To this day not a lot has changed but I do thank you for giving me the opportunity to straighten up and get by, even by the slightest chance. Some time has passed that I just forgot about stuff and went into my paradise which was a fantastic place that I wish one day to have as my home. You told me that I could have anything I ever wanted, that all I had to do was take the path of education and get an extremely high-paying job and that's what I'm going to do. I was also thinking of doing some changes for the better, but I don't know yet we'll have to see in due time. I send my regards that I have grown up and don't need to be taught anymore. I now need to experience my own turn of events.

FREEDOM

Vincent "Rabbit" Wiggins

Jimmy, I wish you the best of success with your book. You inspire me by the way you contribute to the community you serve. I know that you will continue to mentor young people. You once were a menace to society, now you are truly an asset to it.

I'm ashamed of the crimes I committed. I'm praying to God that my physical freedom will one day come.

Jimmy came and visited me on July 5, 2021, in the County Jail—23 years since I saw Jimmy get arrested in front of my home in Tustin. Soon after that, I was arrested myself at the age of 21 for a series of crimes I committed due to gang life. I'm hoping that someday I'll be able to live outside of these prison walls and do some good for the community as Jimmy has.

Through my incarceration, we didn't lose contact, and I wish I could be there for my friend, my brother. I admire Jimmy's dedication and determination to get his book done.

I've been working on my story as well. I believe that as human beings, individually, we all have a story to tell. What led me to prison was that I was an emotional wreck, my mentality was warped, and the choices that I was making on the daily kept the jailhouse doors revolving.

Today, the doors have finally stopped turning. When I was given two life sentences plus 10 years, I didn't think prison would change me. Now I am humbled and I thank

God that prison did change me. I've liberated myself from the criminal lifestyle and it feels good. My life story doesn't end here in prison. Daily, I'm preparing my life for the next chapter. I'm going to call it "Chapter Freedom!"

AFTERWORD

Frostee Rucker

Igrew up across the street from Slim on Mitchell Avenue in Tustin. My sister Monica, who we called MoMo, became good friends with Jimmy, even though my mom did her best to keep us from hanging out with him and his friends.

Jimmy wasn't hard to spot, a 6'2 white boy in a predominantly black gang is always something that will catch an eye. Seeing Slim was a daily happening for me but catching him smiling was a rare occurrence. He always held a straight, hard face. The chilling stories I heard about him never made me cross him. I would be lying if I said that he didn't intimidate me or others. To kids my age, he was like a character from an American Western. In Tustin, we didn't have a Jesse James—we had a Jimmy Rumsey.

I often sit back and think about where my life could have taken me. Growing up, I was all football. I wanted to become a professional and since '93 it was all I dreamed of becoming. Being on the field was a place I felt safe. No nagging sisters, no mom with chores, and no gang activity. That was my escape.

After football practice, the real game was looking out for where Slim and his friends would be waiting for me. Jimmy and his friends would see me walking home from practice and I'd hear, "Get him!" Then the chase was on. If they caught me, I'd receive the worst dead legs from them punching me. I was young, so at this point, they were just messing with me. It was all out of love. I like to think they're part of the reason why I became such a good running back growing up.

To be real though, the fear of getting jumped in their gang wasn't on my mind most of the time because Slim spared me. Every time anyone would mention wanting to "put Lil Frost on the set" it never happened. Slim would usually say something like, "Na, he's not ready."

The guy with the hardened face who rarely smiled protected me.

He was like a big brother. He knew then that I had a passion and a dream, and he did what he could to make sure professional football was a goal I was able to attain.

When the news broke that Slim had been shot, I wasn't shocked at all. It went with the territory. But when I found out how severe it was and that he was shot at point-blank range, I could hear in my sister's cry that we were going to lose Slim for good. The concept of death never really had been put out in the open for me like that up until then.

Slim had just become a new father to a daughter and now this. I realized how life could change in an instant. I heard that he miraculously survived, but I hadn't seen Slim in a long time. I had gone to play football, my sister moved away, and most of the guys that hung out on the block either went to jail or disappeared.

By the time I attended the University of Southern California, years had passed when I received a random call. It was Slim! Without hesitation, I invited him to one of our football games.

When I first saw him again, he was still recovering from the gunshot, but he was a changed person, mentally and spiritually. It was a complete 180-degree lifestyle change. I could tell that he possessed a different attitude. He said to me that he was in the process of starting his life over. With his children and his wife Tasha beside him, he told me things I had never known about him, which he wrote down in this book. What Slim considered normal growing up was other people's fears and other people's traumas.

Before the game was about to start, Slim told me that he was grateful for a second chance to live and to be here watching me play college football.

Over the years that I played in college at USC, I always had him around. I was just a kid from Tustin and people from there stuck together. It felt normal and right to have him on the sidelines.

Because Jimmy protected me and spared me from getting jumped into the gang, I wanted to share with him the great moments of my life. As I got older and was drafted into the NFL, those moments never stopped. The heartfelt conversations we had together grew ever more inspiring. Slim had to overcome a lot during his recovery. He moved out of Tustin and was starting a new life in the Inland Empire for the sake of his family. He had to redefine his purpose in life. I witnessed it all. And he never blamed anyone for his problems. His gratitude for a chance to live a second life gave Slim meaning.

In many of our long conversations, Slim would say to me

how he was going to "give back." If he could help change just one person's life, he said that he would feel better.

Throughout the years, Slim has been working through Project Kinship and has contributed to positive change for the communities that he and his family are a part of.

Slim was always a leader, and now he serves a new group of youths. His gratitude for life has worn off on me. I'm grateful that he spared me and I'm thankful we have someone like Slim in this world to help kids spare themselves. God bless.

Tustin Up -
Frostee Rucker
USC National Champion 03, 04 and Graduate
91st pick in the 2006 NFL Draft
13-year Professional Football Career - Cincinnati Bengals,
    Cleveland Browns, Arizona Cardinals, Oakland Raiders
Founder of The Frostee's Challenge

ACKNOWLEDGMENTS

The completion of this book would not have happened if not for the special people in my life. First and foremost, I would be remiss if I did not thank God for the blessings he has given me. I thank Him for his amazing grace and favor in my life.

Thank you to my mom for being there for me along my journey. Although the journey was not easy for either of us, you did your best to raise me with the life you were given. I sincerely appreciate all you sacrificed for me. Mom, thank you for loving me and for doing your best.

Thank you to Mr. Patterson, aka Pops! You are a rare breed. You and your family came into my life when I was ready to give up on mine. You welcomed me into your home even after I brought trouble to your doorstep on multiple occasions. Mr. Patterson, you always saw the "good in me" even when I didn't see the good in myself. Your acts of kindness toward me gave me hope. There is no way I could ever repay you and Mrs. Patterson for all you did for me. Mr. and Mrs. Patterson, I love you!

Thank you to Frostee. Watching you chase your dreams from youth football to high school to college and then to the NFL was amazing to witness. You are an inspiration to me. Frostee, I am forever grateful to you and proud of you. I love you, lil bro!

Thank you to the co-founders of Project Kinship, Steve and Mary. You both blessed me by allowing me to fulfill one of my dreams—having the opportunity to work with the youth in my hometown. Not only am I thankful for Project Kinship but I am thankful for all the great organizations serving those in need. The work isn't easy, but it's worth it.

I would also like to shout out to the staff and students in the Santa Ana Unified School District, Valley High School, Lorin Griset Academy, Century High School and REACH Academy. Never in my wildest dreams did I imagine I would be working in the schools. I have met so many great people in this field. It has been an honor and privilege to work with all of you. To all of the youth who struggle, don't give up on your education, dreams, or yourself—anything is possible! Thank you for allowing me into your lives.

Thank you to Lil Ron. I miss you. You were a true friend to me. I often wonder how life would have been different if you had lived. I am sorry that I introduced you to my homies. You were one of the good guys and your life was cut too short. Until we meet again, you will stay in my heart forever.

Thank you to my good friend, Vince "Rabbit" Wiggins I thank God for your authentic friendship. I am blessed to have you in my life. Your fingerprints are on the work that I do every day with the youth. I look forward to us reuniting when you gain your freedom so that we can work together to make a difference.

Thank you to Courtney. Who knew when you walked into my mom's house with your jokes that you would one day literally save my life? Thank you for not walking away from me that day in the Circle K parking lot. Thank you for holding my head and talking to me. Without you, I would not be here. Thank you, my brother. I love you.

And last but most definitely not least, I would like to thank the love of my life, Tasha. You never gave up on me and always stayed solid in my corner since the first day that we met. I've never had to question your love for me. The family that we have built together has given me purpose and a reason to hold on when I wanted to give up. I am so blessed and grateful to have you as my wife, soulmate, and best friend. Thank you for loving me and being patient with me. I love you, Mrs. Natasha Rumsey! There's no me without you!

ABOUT THE AUTHOR

Jimmy Rumsey works with at-promise youth in California's Santa Ana Unified School District as a Restorative Practice Intervention Specialist. His own life experiences with a dysfunctional family, incarceration, violence, and gangs have helped him serve as a positive mentor to youth who have endured similar life circumstances. He is highly respected in the community for his commitment to helping others heal from their own life traumas. His wife, Tasha, stood beside him as he went from being a risk to himself and others to being a valuable contributor to his community. Jimmy is also a devoted father of five children.

You can reach Jimmy through his website at
www.slimchancesbook.com

Made in the USA
Columbia, SC
09 April 2023

6c3ea132-0478-4deb-9489-400db97a1ca1R01